FORGIVENESS

HOW TO GET ALONG WITH EVERYBODY ALL THE TIME!

**HAROLD VAUGHAN
and T.P. JOHNSTON**

Copyright © 1992 by Harold D. Vaughan
Printed in the United States of America
ISBN: 0-942889-07-X

Christ Life Publications
P.O. Box 399
Vinton, VA 24179

PREFACE

If the title on the cover seems too promising, wait until you finish the book to make your judgment. The Bible does not promise others will always get along with us, but it does tell us how we should respond to them. That's what this book is all about: **our** part in getting along with others. The Scripture is clear in teaching us our responsibility.

Viewing Christianity in our day, I can think of no greater truth that needs to be practiced than forgiveness. So many are in bondage because of bitterness. Deep hurts, broken promises, awful crimes, and piercing wounds have left tremendous scars and devastating divisions. The Bible prescribes the cure in such cases: forgiveness and reconciliation.

Utopia is not promised in this life. Offenses will come. Sometimes we are the offender, other times we are the offended. When offenses come, we must know and **practice** the truth of forgiveness. Through Calvary forgiveness has become a blessed reality. Healing, liberation, and lasting freedom are yours for the taking. It is our desire that many will be set free by the truth presented in this book.

Contents

Section 1

Granting Forgiveness

Chapter 1

Why Should
I Forgive?

The way we treat our fellow man is a direct gauge of our relationship with God. The Lord Jesus takes personally the way we relate to others. *"Inasmuch as ye have done it unto one of the least of these my brethren, ye have done it unto me" (Matt. 25:40).* Consequently, to be at odds with a fellow Christian spells double trouble: not only are we at odds with our brother, but we are also at odds with Jesus in him!

Everybody is talking about "priorities." Whether it's in the business world, politics, education, or Christian ministry, "priorities" is a popular buzz-word. Depending on the group and its objectives, the priorities will surely vary. But what is the foremost priority of the Christian life according to the Bible? What is first on God's agenda?

Jesus spelled it out, clearly. *"Therefore if thou bring thy gift to the altar, and there rememberest that thy brother hath aught against thee; leave there thy gift before the altar, and go thy way; **first be reconciled** to thy brother, and then come and offer thy gift" (Matt. 5:23-24).*

Reconciliation is God's priority for you and me. It precedes giving, service, and sacrifice. So important is reconciliation that Jesus said "leave your gift" and "first be reconciled." Before giving and serving, our Lord demands reconciliation. But why?

The Old Testament declared that any high priest who touched a dead carcass was ceremonially unclean. Once defiled, he was not allowed to carry out his priestly duties until he had gone through a purification process. Touching a dead carcass would not of itself prevent the priest from carrying out his duties. Efficiency was not the issue. He could have easily gone through the motions, but his service was unacceptable to God because he was personally contaminated. Here is a worthy principle: the acceptability of any gift is determined by the acceptability of the giver. If the giver is unfit, the gift is unacceptable, even abominable in God's sight. God will not accept a gift if the giver is personally contaminated by unreconciled relationships.

That's why God said we must first attempt to be reconciled. Broken relationships so contaminate us before God that our service is unacceptable. We must first seek reconciliation. As Christians, our vertical relationship with God is affected by our horizontal relationships with our fellow man. If we are to stabilize our relationship with God, often we must begin by first stabilizing horizontal relationships.

The word reconciliation means "to be at peace with." Our fallen nature was at enmity with God, but the Lord Jesus reconciled us to God by His death on the Cross. The enmity is gone once you're saved; you are at peace with God. Reconciliation means putting things right when things have gone wrong. When it comes to our attention that we have offended someone, intentionally or unintentionally, knowingly or unknowingly, willingly or unwillingly, then our responsibility is to drop everything and go to the offended party. Then in humility and sincerity, the attempt at restoration is made. The response of the offended party may be positive or negative. But once we obey God we are free, and his response is between him and God.

Scripture reveals the importance of forgiveness and reconciliation. To be "on the outs" on earth means we are out of touch with heaven. We are admonished to keep open communication lines in marriage "lest our prayers be hindered." For example, when you're not on speaking terms with your mate, you are not on speaking terms with God. Herein lies the root of much spiritual sickness. Few people realize how unforgiveness, hurt feelings, and adverse relationships dramatically affect our relationship with God. The Apostle John said, *"For he that loveth not his brother whom he hath seen, how can he love God whom he hath not seen?" (1 John 4:20).* In other words, if we cannot properly relate to human beings, how can we pretend to be rightly relating to God?

Jesus said "**first be reconciled**." If this matter of reconciliation and forgiveness is first on Jesus' list, then it must be first on ours as well. The importance of forgiveness will be clearly seen in subsequent chapters where the consequences of not forgiving are discussed in more detail.

Questions For Personal Growth

Why Should I Forgive?

1. The "First" directives in Scripture focus on God's priorities for our lives. Describe why forgiving our offenders is on God's priority list for us.

2. What is the essential meaning of "reconciliation"? Discern if there is currently anyone with whom your relationship could not be described by this definition of reconciliation.

Chapter 2

What is Forgiveness?

Misconceptions concerning forgiveness abound. Its nature is so radical that forgiveness is an abstract ideal in the minds of many. Often we can come closer to understanding what something is by defining what it is not. Here are a few of the misconceptions concerning forgiveness.

Forgiveness is not an emotion. In fact, our feelings are quite irrelevant! Jesus prayed, "Father forgive them," while suspended on Calvary's Cross. Physically tortured, spiritually tormented, and mentally tried, the Lord Jesus made a choice to forgive. His request was obviously an act of His will, not just an emotional outburst. Stephen, while being stoned to death, prayed and asked God to forgive his bloodthirsty accusers—not to lay that sin to their charge. Forgiveness in its initial stage is definitely not an emotion and can be granted despite feelings.

Forgiveness is not forgetting. How often has it been said, "If you didn't forget it, you really didn't forgive"? That's the most absurd counsel that could be given! It is humanly impossible to blot out unwanted memories at will. Almighty God is the only One who has the ability to willingly forget. Only He could say, *"I will forgive their iniquity, and I will remember their sin no more" (Jer. 31:34).* On the human level, forgetting has nothing to do with forgiving. We've all had things happen to us that will never be forgotten while on this planet, but fortunately, that has nothing to do with forgiveness. Time will not heal all hurts, but forgiveness is the doorway that puts you well on your way in the healing process. Once forgiveness is granted, recurring thoughts about the episode may, and probably will, return. This does not mean you were insincere. You will learn how to turn these thoughts to prayer later in this book. Although you may not be able to completely forget, the frequency these thoughts come to mind will decrease once you decide to forgive. As you practice the freedom of forgiveness, the intervals of re-membrance will lengthen. And when the incident does come to mind, you will know how to handle it.

Forgiveness is not shrugging off the offense. It is not just letting it slide or taking a neutral position. In fact, it is impossible to be neutral and God expects you to respond properly. As we shall see, forgiveness is far more than doing nothing.

Forgiveness is not asking God to forgive the person who hurt you. That is commendable, but it is not forgiveness. In fact, you could only pray, "Father, forgive them for they know not what they do" with meaning after you have forgiven them yourself. When Jesus prayed He had no malice in His heart. The crucifixion was "the cup" that He had to drink. When He prayed on the Cross He was not attempting to empty His soul of anger; it was an honest prayer of concern.

Forgiveness is not asking God to forgive you for

being hurt or angry. We need to take responsibility for our attitudes and actions, but this is secondary. If someone offended me it is a must that I forgive that particular someone. I must deal with God about my resentment, but I also must deal with the person who hurt me.

Forgiveness is not rationalizing or understanding why the person acted toward you as he did. Why they did what they did is irrelevant. Understanding the reasons for what they have done is not necessary, neither is it forgiveness.

What, then, is forgiveness? First, **forgiveness is a choice.** It is nothing less than a decisive act of the will. Jesus spoke of a certain king who took account of his servants and found one that owed him millions of dollars. The king commanded that the slave, his family, and his belongings be sold in order to pay the debt. The servant pleaded for more time and told the king he would pay him back. But he could never have paid him back. He was so far in debt that repayment was out of the question. Nevertheless, his pleading paid off. The king forgave him all the debt and set him free. This forgiven, liberated servant promptly went out and arrested a fellow slave. He took this fellow slave by the throat and demanded payment of the few dollars owed him. The indebted servant fell down on his knees and begged for a little time in which to pay the debt. This was in the realm of possibility; in time he could have paid him back. But the servant wouldn't listen, and he had him thrown into debtor's prison. Here is a man who, released from a staggering debt, refused to forgive his fellow slave an insignificant sum. The king called his servant in. After calling him a wicked servant, the master harshly rebuked him and delivered him to the tormentors until he paid all that was due. Jesus concluded by warning that the heavenly Father will do the same thing to us if we refuse to forgive those who wrong us.

This story teaches us that forgiveness is a decision to release others from the debts they owe us. When we refuse to forgive, we put the unforgiven party in debtor's prison. Let me illustrate. Suppose I was your pastor, and somehow I offended you. Perhaps I made a decision you didn't agree with or didn't recognize some sacrifice you made for the church. Perhaps I failed to visit you while you were sick. That offense is all you think about when you see me. You have bound me and put me in debtor's prison. I may even come and ask for forgiveness, but unless you release me from that debt, others can be blessed and helped, but I cannot help you. In your eyes everything I do is tainted by that one act of injury. In refusing to forgive me, you bind me from being what God wants me to be in your life. When you fail to forgive, refuse to release from debt, you put others in debtor's prison. It may not be a physical prison, but it is certainly real. Your holding those offenses against me lands me in a position of debtor from which I cannot escape without your consent. You have bound me in debtor's prison.

When I started to seriously consider forgiveness, I made a shocking discovery. It came to my attention that most people have an "accounts receivable" book. I am not referring to a black book in a businessman's desk drawer. This "accounts receivable" book is filed away in the human heart. Every time someone offends us, down it goes. They owe me. I am holding a debt against them. This is not an "I-owe-you." It's a "You-owe-me"! When your mate crosses you, down it goes: "I'll remember that." If the pastor offends us, it is promptly entered on the balance sheet. When our children embarrass us, down it goes. "I'll remember that next time they want to go out for ice cream!" When people wrong us, we place them in the "accounts receivable" file. They are in debt to us. They owe us.

Many would be willing to forgive if their transgressors would apologize. Good news! You do not have to wait for an apology to forgive someone. Wicked scoffers were mocking Jesus while He hung on the Cross. None of them offered an apology, yet Jesus prayed, "Father, forgive them." How other people respond or fail to respond makes no difference; you can release people from their debts whenever you choose. You need not wait for an apology.

Forgiveness is a decision to shred the "You-Owe-Me" list. It is a deliberate choice to release people from the debt they owe you. Are you living in a spiritual vacuum? Do you have a "You-Owe-Me" list? Here's how to shred it. Go to the Lord in prayer and tell Him that you are making some choices to forgive. Here's an example: "Lord, I am making a decision to forgive my friend for breaking a confidence. Lord, it hurt me, but I will never hold it against him again. I release him from that debt. I forgive him." Continue to pray and don't stop until you have shredded your entire list. Every resentment against your parents, children, family members, neighbors, church members, employers, and employees, should be confessed and forsaken. Ron Lee Davis in his book, Mistreated writes:

> Some years ago, a millionaire—let's call him Mr. Yale—owned a lot in an exclusive residential area of a large city. This lot presented an unusual problem because it was only a couple yards wide by nearly a hundred feet long. Clearly, there was nothing he could do with such an oddly proportioned piece of real estate but sell it to one of the neighbors on either side. So Mr. Yale went first to Mr. Smith, the neighbor on the east side of the lot,

and asked if he would be interested in buying it.

"Well," said Mr. Smith, "I really wouldn't have much use for it. But I'll tell you what, since you're in something of a bind, I'd be willing to take it off your hands—purely as a favor, of course." Then he named a ridiculously low price.

"A favor, you say!" Yale exploded. "Why, that's not even one-tenth what the lot is worth!"

"That's all it's worth to me, and that's my offer."

Yale stormed out and went to see the neighbor on the west side, Mr. Jones. To Yale's dismay, Jones bettered the previous offer by only a few dollars. "Look, Yale," Jones said smugly, "I've got you over a barrel and you know it. You can't sell that lot to anyone else and you can't build on it. So there's my offer. Take it or leave it."

"So you think I'm over a barrel?" Yale retorted. "I'll show you no one can cheat me!"

"What are you going to do?"

Yale grinned maliciously. "You just wait!"

Within a few days, the embittered millionaire hired an architect and a contractor to build one of the strangest houses ever conceived. Only five feet wide and running the full length of his property, Yale's house was little more than a row of claustrophobic rooms, each barely able to accommodate a stick of furniture. As the house went up, the neighbors complained that the bizarre structure would blight the neighborhood, but city officials could find no code or regulation to disallow it.

When it was finished, Yale moved into his uncomfortable and impractical house, a self-condemned man in a prison of revenge. There he stayed for many years. Finally, he died there. The house, which became known in the neighborhood as "Spite House," still stands as a monument to one man's hate.[1]

Unforgiveness is a two-way street. If you decide to put someone in debtor's prison, God will do the same to you! Jesus said His heavenly Father would bind and deliver you to the tormentors. Once unforgiveness occurs, the Lord places you in debtor's prison, in a spiritual vacuum. He will not forgive you until you choose to forgive others. Unconfessed sin completely hinders your spiritual life. You can't pray, witness, or worship. Your spiritual life will shrivel and die. This is the reap-what-you-sow principle. God responds to you just like you respond to others. Unforgiveness imprisons not only those indebted to us, but sentences us to the same place we have put others. When you forgive, you set a prisoner free and then you discover you were that prisoner!

Reconciliation must be initiated by the person to whom God speaks. It is not a matter of meeting someone halfway or waiting for them to approach you. Once God calls a conflict to your attention, leave your gift and go your way and seek reconciliation. Two ladies in a church were at odds, and everyone knew it. The Lord spoke to one of them. She went to the other and, by humbling herself, was able to get the conflict resolved. When God speaks, you must respond. You don't have to search for the incidents; God will point them out. Then, after God speaks, you must be the one who initiates reconciliation.

Years ago I took some clothes to a local dry-cleaners. Not only did I take clothes to the cleaners, I got taken to the cleaners on the same trip! After getting home with the clothes, I discovered the pants were torn and a necktie was wrecked. "No problem," I thought, "I'll just take them back and get reimbursed." So I gathered up my damaged clothes and went back to the dry-cleaners. I showed the clerk my ruined garments and expected repayment. However, the clerk informed me that the manager took care of these incidents, and he was not available. "No problem," I said, "When will he be in?" She gave me a time and I went back, but he still was not in. I am a little slow in catching on, but after five return visits I began to see an emerging pattern! They intended to beat me out of any reimbursement and I was furious! My first thought was to take out a newspaper advertisement warning the public against that business establishment. Then I found out that was illegal. Next, I thought about printing up a handbill and warning all potential customers by stationing myself on the sidewalk immediately outside the cleaners. But I didn't have time for that, so I contacted the Better Business Bureau. By now you can see that I was angry, very angry. I had been cheated. I was getting nowhere on the human level so I decided on a spiritual attack. The verse came to mind, *"Vengeance is mine, saith the Lord. I will repay."* So I prayed, "Lord, let them have it!" Every time I drove by, I would glance over to see whether the place had been struck by lightning the night before! I was really mad. I had sought justice but did not find it. That is often the case in this fallen world. There is nothing wrong with seeking justice, but most often you will not find it. I was left with two choices: get bitter or forgive. Being bitter is sin, so I chose (I didn't feel like it) to forgive. I released that debt and turned them over to God. I never got reimbursed and I never received an apology, but that does not matter now. That decision to forgive released me from my prison of bitterness.

Questions for Personal Growth

What is Forgiveness?

1. When our minds accept wrong concepts, to that degree, we are deceived. From the list of misconceptions concerning forgiveness, which one(s) have been a part of your thinking?

2. If possible, relate these faulty views to specific people and events in your life. Purpose to reject wrong thinking regarding forgiveness, asking God to give you discernment.

3. Wrong thinking, when believed and acted upon, brings destructive consequences. What harsh chastening does God bring when we fail to forgive others?

[1]Ron Lee Davis, *Mistreated* (Portland, Oregon: Multnomah, 1989), pp. 19-20.

Chapter 3

What if I Don't Want to Forgive?

While it is true that forgiveness is costly, unforgiveness is even more costly. In the final analysis, they are costly in entirely different ways. Though forgiveness is painful in the initial stages, the ultimate end is healing. Unforgiveness produces immediate bitterness and spiritual barrenness now, but ultimately it leads to a host of other destructive consequences. What are the results of that corrosive culprit called bitterness?

The first consequence of not forgiving is spiritual death. As we have already seen, when we don't forgive others, God doesn't forgive us. The seriousness of this cannot be overstated. Unforgiveness is unforgivable! A person who **cannot** forgive is a person who has not been forgiven. When God in mercy saves a lost soul, He implants within that soul the ability to forgive. I am not saying a Christian is incapable of harboring resentment. But "cannot forgive" and "will not forgive" are two different things. A true Christian **can** forgive when he chooses. Unforgiveness in a child of God is an awful thing. It kills every ounce of spiritual vitality. How often have you witnessed the deterioration and plummet of a bitter Christian? He who will not forgive breaks the bridge over which he himself must pass. As long as he covers his sin he cannot prosper.

Mark makes a definite connection between unforgiveness and unanswered prayer. *"What things soever ye desire, when ye pray, believe that ye receive them, and ye shall have them. And when ye stand praying, forgive, if ye have aught against any: that your Father also which is in heaven may forgive you your trespasses" (Mark 11:24-25).* This great promise regarding prayer is followed by a condition and a serious warning: *"forgive... that your Father which is in heaven may forgive you your trespasses."* Unforgiveness bars God from even hearing our prayers. The Psalmist said, *"If I regard iniquity in my heart, the Lord will not hear me" (Ps. 66:18).* If you choose not to obey by forgiving, then God chooses not to listen when you pray! How much unanswered prayer is there because of unforgiveness in the heart? If you have an unanswered prayer list, the first place to start checking is your unforgiveness list.

God's presence is not sensed when unforgiveness is present. The Psalmist stated, *"In thy presence is fulness of joy" (Ps. 16:11).* God hides Himself when we develop ingrown eyeballs and wallow in pity and harbor resentment. Focused on self, we lose all sense of God. As earlier stated, we are shut up in a spiritual vacuum. The absence of God's personal presence means no joy.

Bitterness not only kills the person who harbors it, but infects others with its deadly poison. The defiling fountain of bitterness is not content to remain alone; it seeps out and poisons everything it touches. Bitter preachers pollute congregations. The sins of the parents often are passed on to the children. When Christian leaders are mistreated they must guard against bitterness. If not, their own offspring are likely to grow up despising God, the faith, and the church. When offended church members spill out their deadly poison at home, it is no wonder their children are cynical and cold toward Christianity. Bitter church members carry a tainted message to a watching world. *"Follow peace with all men,"* we are exhorted, " *" . . . lest any root of bitterness springing up trouble you and thereby many be defiled" (Hebrews 12:14,15).* The picture here is not a placid pool, but a gushing, corrupt spring! Though some try to hold it in, the acid of bitterness is sure to eat through the container walls and contaminate others.

Indulging in the sin of unforgiveness not only puts a stumbling block before one's family, but also offends the unsaved and weaker Christians as well. Romans 14 warns of putting a stumbling block in someone else's path. Better to suffer loss than offend others. Jesus stated it would be better to be thrown overboard in the ocean with a millstone about your neck than offend a little child. Infecting a child with attitudes of hatred surely fits in the category of offending a little one. How many have been hindered because of the stumbling block of unforgiveness?

Another destructive consequence of unforgiveness is emotional depression. We are told that a large portion of Americans suffer from this problem. Newsweek magazine carried an article entitled *"The Mental State of the Union "* in which they reported 20 percent of the adult population suffered some type of psychiatric disorder. The article stated that approximately ten million suffer from depression. Certainly there can be a variety of causes for this condition, but who could deny that in many cases depression is caused by pent-up hostility from broken relationships.

The human spirit is our greatest asset when healthy, but a handicap when broken. *"The spirit of man will sustain his infirmity; but a wounded spirit who can bear" (Prov. 18:14).* The will must be exercised to forgive when those harsh blows hit because a damaged spirit is intolerable.

A wounded spirit can be a debilitating force, especially when bitterness becomes an obsession. Mental side effects naturally follow in the wake of depression. Irrationality, the inability to think clearly, is one cognitive impairment that often results. The mind is short-circuited and the thinking processes become warped. Often the mind continually dwells on the same things. Over and over the same trash is rehearsed. It can become so severe that one is totally incapacitated.

Improper relationships are also significant because of the unnecessary stress they bring. Tension, nervousness, and various types of mental illness are a few of the adverse results of disobedience in this area. The human body is not designed to house these repercussions. Praise the Lord for giving us clear steps for seeking to resolve conflicts.

In addition, there are physical consequences of not forgiving. The human body cannot function properly with a spiritual cancer eating away at it. Medical science now claims that anger, bitterness, and hatred adversely affect the human body. Many illnesses, including heart disease, high blood pressure, ulcers, and a whole array of physical disorders may be caused by this sin. It is only natural that a man's spiritual and emotional state should affect the health of his body. *"A merry heart doeth good like a medicine: but a broken spirit drieth the bones" (Prov. 17:22).* Bitterness is not an isolated occurrence; it is a way of life that constantly drains the body.

Dale Carnegie told the story of a grizzly bear in Yellowstone National Park. Some garbage was piled in a clearing, and the bear came to eat the garbage. The grizzly is probably the most ferocious animal in North America. The grizzly doesn't have many challengers. But while the bear was there eating the garbage, a little skunk came to the clearing. He went to where the bear was eating and began to eat. The skunk was very impudent, but the bear didn't do anything. They shared the food. Why? Because the bear knew the high cost of getting even!

Life is too short to live with the destructive consequences of unforgiveness. It's just not worth it. Obedience brings blessing and one of life's greatest blessings is the inner healing that forgiveness brings. Disobedience in this area, as in any other, carries a price tag. Forgiveness is not a suggestion; it is a commandment. The wonderful thing is that God never requires anything out of you except what His grace puts into you. The Lord never asks us to do anything without giving us the ability to carry it out. Since forgiveness is required, failure to forgive brings negative consequences: *"Be not deceived; God is not mocked: for whatsoever a man soweth, that shall he also reap" (Gal. 6:7).* Aren't you glad for the grace of God which enables you to forgive?

Questions for Personal Growth

What If I Don't Want To Forgive?

1. Briefly list the five consequences of bitterness discussed in this chapter. After each one, note down examples you have observed, either in your own life, or in others' lives.

2. Use examples from the lives of others as a warning to avoid bitterness at all costs in your own life.

3. For those examples from your own life, determine if the causes of them were repented of and set right. If

any were not, purpose that you will deal with them. (It would be wise to complete the reading of this book before proceeding so you understand clearly what God requires to deal with each situation.)

Chapter 4

How Does Unforgiveness Give Ground to Satan?

Christians are quick to decry the works of the devil through the drug crisis, pornography, abortion, secular humanism, and a host of attendant evils. Yet, as much advantage is being gained by Satan through the unforgiving spirits of professing Christians as perhaps through all of these malignant vices combined. Satan knows that men will delve deeply in the mire of overt sin completely on their own with little urging from him. But if he can defeat and mar the testimonies, health, and relationships of believers through unforgiveness, he will manufacture and seize every opportunity possible.

Relationships are the very crucible of life. They are among the most difficult as well as the most enjoyable experiences we have in life. It is impossible to escape relationships. Because we are all sinful by nature as well as by choice, it is only a matter of time before any and every relationship becomes tainted. Perhaps we are deliberately offended, or perhaps we are hurt and disappointed by the failure of the other party to meet our expectations. Relationships all tend to move through at least four levels. Initially, entering into a relationship with another, we tend to see only the good and be very idealistic about the relationship. Soon, however, reality sets in and we begin wondering to ourselves, "Hmm, I didn't realize you were like this." This is quickly followed by feelings of resentment, a feeling that we have been let down profoundly. We find ourselves not liking the way the other person is. And if we are not careful, resentment sours into hatred— a desire to get out of the relationship altogether. But this is not God's way.

Invariably, when we are confronted with the issue of unforgiveness, we find ourselves "pitchfork" Christians. We take these truths and fling them over our shoulders, hoping that so-and-so is listening and will get the point. But we must lay down our pitchforks and allow God's Word to penetrate deeply. Failure to do so will be very costly. Refusing to forgive never ends there. It plunges us into a downward and spiritually destructive spiral.

Ephesians 4:31 details this ruinous plummet. We must appreciate the context of this verse to grasp the gravity of the situation a lack of forgiveness generates. Ephesians 4:26,27 warns: *"Be ye angry, and sin not: let not the sun go down upon your wrath: Neither give place to the devil."*

Allowing the sun to go down on one's wrath simply means that we harbor unforgiveness—we go to bed angry with another. When that happens, the door is left ajar for Satan. Ephesians 4:30 notes that God's Holy Spirit is grieved when we permit this to occur. An unforgiving spirit is the devil's legal campground. It gives him a "place" of entry into our lives where he can begin to war against us from within. Verse 31 gives us the downward spiral: *"Let all bitterness, and wrath, and anger, and clamour, and evil speaking, be put away from you, with all malice."*

Bitterness

Notice carefully the phases of Satan's attack once he is given ground. His first tactic is that of poisoning. Bitterness is a word that simply means poison. Bitterness is the direct result of an unforgiving spirit. A bitter person is simply someone who has been hurt. Someone has wounded him, neglected him, abused him, rejected him, slighted him, cheated him, or at least he feels that these things have happened. Rather than admitting it and going to others to settle it, he harbors the hurt. Like a poison introduced into the body, bitterness is a poison of the soul. The longer it stays the more deeply entrenched it becomes, the more it permeates the entire life. The analogy of a poison in the body is striking. Scripture refers to the "gall of bitterness." Bitterness of soul has now been medically demonstrated to be a factor in cholesistitis or gall bladder disease. It sets up a chemical imbalance in the body which causes cholesterol to precipitate in the form of gall stones. The relationship is direct. Bitterness is an acid poison which eats away its own container.

Occasionally, bitterness is easily spotted, as in the woman who went to her physician and was told that she had rabies. She immediately took out a pen and pad and began writing. The doctor questioned her, wondering if she was writing her last will and testament. Her reply? "No, I'm making out a list of the people I'm going to bite."

More often, bitterness is not on the surface, however. Hebrews 12:15 refers to it as a root. One of the duties of a shepherd in biblical times was to prepare the field for the sheep by carefully digging up any poisonous plants. Failure to do so would result in sick and dead sheep. Likewise, unforgiveness must be removed before it develops roots in the life. **No one can harbor any degree of unforgiveness without becoming bitter.** Bitterness may be masked before others as well as to one's own self. But it always is destructive.

It shuts out the flow of the life of God through our lives. Our prayers are hindered. Our lives become joyless and fruitless. A little girl had been chastened by her mother. Still angry with Mom, she knelt to say her prayers while her mother waited to tuck her in. She prayed for her Dad, her brothers and sister, her aunts, and uncles and grandparents. She said, "Amen," then turned to her mother and announced, "I guess you noticed I left you out." The problem is, she left God out too! Prayers from an unforgiving heart extend no further than the light bulbs. Praise and worship become a mockery. The life is poisoned at the source.

Wrath

Bitterness unresolved eventually results in the next phase of Satan's attack: wrath. Wrath is an interesting word which has the idea of heat connected with it. Wrath is that slow burn inside. It is an inward seething against the offender, a smoldering resentment. The word "resentment" means "to feel again." We actually delight to feel again the hurt and sorrow of wrongs done to us. It provides us a bitter-sweet pleasure. Wrath is the fire set by the initial hurt which was not set right. It is akin to rags tossed in a waste can and set aflame, then put into a closed closet. It just slowly but surely burns.

Anger

When the closed door is flung open, the rags of smoldering wrath burst into flame. That is anger, the third stage of Satan's assault on the unforgiving soul. Something will happen which will reveal the wrath and bitterness in the life, and the individual finds himself in a fit of anger. Differences that are less than minor may develop into full scale war on a personal level. Such only reveals that a root of bitterness was there which set off the conflagration. Anger has the idea of something outward and open. Perhaps you have had the experience of surprising even yourself with an outburst of anger. You may not have known how irritable (smoldering) you were inside until something set you off. This is likely the result of a root of bitterness displaying its fruit. We like to stonewall and wear a facade, pretending there is nothing wrong. But it is impossible to purify the water by painting the pump. Bitterness eventually finds an outlet in anger.

Clamour

When anger bursts forth, it frequently is followed by clamour. You begin to verbalize. The word itself entails speech. Maybe you shout, perhaps you argue at a high decibel level, or simply cry. The poison has so corrupted your soul that it has filled you and overflows through the tongue. The Bible describes such a tongue as a fire, a world of iniquity.

Evil Speaking

Clamour soon turns to evil speaking. Words are spoken which you never imagined you would utter. "I hate you!"

"I wish you were dead." "I'm sorry we ever had you for a child." "I hope I never see you again." Or that too often repeated phrase, "I want a divorce." Things are said which we do not mean. It is all the result of an unforgiving spirit, a bitterness that was never resolved.

Malice

Finally, evil speaking boils into malice. Malice is the desire to harm someone. Do not ever be deceived as to the depths to which Satan can take you when you yield him ground through failing to forgive. You may punch someone out, or take a gun or knife or some other weapon and threaten or actually harm him. You may destroy someone financially. You may so maliciously slander him and assassinate his character that his reputation is demolished.

Satan is systematically demolishing the lives of many people through their unforgiveness. Alexander Pope said, "Sin is a monster of such awful mien [appearance] that to be hated needs but to be seen, but seen too oft, familiar with face, we first endure, then pity, then embrace." Forgiveness is the basis of our relationship with God through Jesus Christ. Failure to forgive others is thus a serious sin and an affront to God. And this sin especially will take us farther than we had planned to go, keep us longer than we had planned to stay, and cost us more than we had planned to pay. There are only two choices. Either we dig up the root of bitterness by God's grace, or it will finally ruin us.

Questions for Personal Growth

How Does Unforgiveness Give Ground To Satan?

1. Carefully read Ephesians 4:26-32. Take note again of the downward stages through which Satan leads an

individual who has failed to forgive someone. Are any of these stages being evidenced in your life because of your unforgiveness?

2. If so, recall the authors' statement that forgiveness is a deliberate choice of the mind and will. Realize that you have yielded ground to Satan. Confess this to God, ask His forgiveness. Pray in the Name and through the Blood of Christ that God will restore to you the ground you have delivered to Satan.

Chapter 5

You've Convinced Me – But Where Do I Start?

Circumstances will determine the proper approach. The Bible gives crystal clear guidelines for most situations and principles that cover every situation. When there has been an obvious offense, "go and be reconciled." In these situations we are called to be peacemakers, to go in lowliness with the intent of restoration. The proper way is to take the blame for your wrong actions, reactions, or attitudes. This is not the time to attack the other party. That's between him and God. Your need is to take responsibility for your offenses. There are times when we need "to go" (more will be said concerning this in Section 2: Seeking Forgiveness).

Then, there are times when we must forgive. Jesus said in Mark 11:25, *"And when ye stand praying, forgive, if you have aught against any: that your Father also...may forgive you your trespasses."* This includes those fleshly acts that are sure to rise up in all of us sooner or later. We don't need to go running to everyone about every little thing. When minor points arise, just make a choice to release that debt and get on with your praying. Don't get bogged down with trivial offenses. Grow up in Christ! Deal with it in your heart and move on.

When I began a serious study of forgiveness in preparation for a sermon, God began to speak to my own heart. Honestly, I was unaware of the bitterness and resentment in my soul. However, the lack of peace and anxiety caused me to recognize something was wrong. The longer I studied the more convicted I became. One day I took a walk in our back yard and decided the time had come to make some hard decisions. On this day I prayed like I had never prayed before. "Lord, I am choosing right now to forgive this person who embarrassed me in front of my friends when I was a child. It hurt, Lord, but I release him from that debt . . . . Lord, my friend hurt me and caused me trouble by breaking a confidence. I am making a decision to release him from that debt. . . . Lord, here are some people who lied to me. It hurt but I choose right now to forgive them. I'll never hold it against them again." It took me thirty minutes to shred my "You-owe-me" list. When I released them, God released me and I came out of the back yard with the joy of the Lord in my heart again!

I recall another case where a lady had been offended by a former pastor. He was unaware of his offence. In fact, he was offended. God spoke to this lady about the unforgiveness in her heart. She chose to forgive her former pastor for this offense. Later that night she called him and told him that she had forgiven him. Remember, he was unaware of any problem on his part. He did not respond positively. In cases like this when we need to forgive, it may not be necessary to inform the people of our decision. In fact, if they are not asking for forgiveness we should keep it between ourselves and God. If they are unrepentant it will not do any good to tell them we have forgiven them. Remember Jesus' example when He prayed, "Father, forgive them." He kept it between Him and His heavenly Father. Nothing was said to those who crucified Him; all the talk was directed toward God.

In the event you can't settle it in your heart, you may need to approach the other party. Matthew chapter eighteen gives us the procedure to follow when we have been offended and gracious confrontation is required. *"Moreover if thy brother shall trespass against thee, go and tell him his fault between thee and him alone: if he shall hear thee, thou hast gained thy brother. But if he will not hear thee, then take with thee one or two more, that in the mouth of two or three witnesses every word may be established. And if he shall neglect to hear them, tell it unto the church: but if he neglect to hear the church, let him be unto thee as an heathen man and a publican"* (*Matt. 18:15-17*).

When you're offended, notice the Bible says you are to go to "him alone." Don't speak to another soul; approach your offender directly. Isn't that hard to do? Someone said, "your tongue is in a wet place and it's easy for it to slip!" Something on the inside (the flesh) wants to broadcast your hurt to everyone. Obedience to this point is essential if we are to avoid causing others to take up offenses for us against those who have wronged us. Many church splits could be prevented by speaking of our offenses only to our offender and no one else. It's also vital that we refuse the reports people seek to give us about wrongs done to them by others than ourselves. How we need the control of the Holy Spirit to keep our tongue in check by speaking only to the one who has wronged us. If this fails to resolve the difficulty, the Scripture instructs us to take one or two people and go back to the offender. They are there to help mediate the problem. They also are witnesses to what is said. This text is dealing with Christians. If one or two witnesses doesn't work, the Scripture states the next step is to bring it before the church. The erring brother is to be publicly exposed. The purpose is to restore the offender. This is God's way of bringing repentance to the sinning brother and maintaining purity within the Body. It is not easy, but it is necessary. Imagine how much better off churches and Christians would be if this practice was obeyed.

Then, there are occasions when we need to ask God alone for forgiveness. Suppose you have entertained negative thoughts about someone. They have not really offended you, and they are not aware of your thoughts. If they have not done anything, and they don't know you have mental barriers erected against them, you don't need to go to them. You need to go to God and ask His forgiveness. Never go to someone in your church and say, "You aren't aware of it, but I have had evil thoughts about you. Would you please forgive me for thinking that you are the biggest clod in the whole congregation?" That type of confession is never warranted. Likewise, lustful thoughts about another person should be confessed to God alone. Never say, "I have resented you," or "I have had lustful thoughts about you and I want you to forgive me." You are to approach the other party **only** when he or she knows about the situation. Sharing unknown thoughts or feelings may create thoughts in the other party's mind that were not there previously. This can create more problems—resentment, for example. Also, private lustful thoughts expressed openly may generate the same thoughts in another mind and stimulate an immoral relationship. When others are unaware and unoffended, forgiveness should be sought solely from God since our sin is between us and Him.

There is another time when forgiveness needs to be granted, and that is when others come to us seeking to right a wrong. It is extremely important to properly express forgiveness verbally. When someone approaches you and apologizes, never say, "Oh, forget it" or "That's alright, it doesn't matter." The appropriate response is, "I forgive you." Those three words are what a guilty conscience needs to hear. Our response should be a means of release to our offender. When asked for forgiveness, never be bashful about saying that blessed trinity of words, "I forgive you."

Questions for Personal Growth

You've Convinced Me - But Where Do I Start?

1. Why is obedience to God's directive to go to an offender and talk with him alone so important?
2. Name two types of circumstances in which forgiveness should be sought only from the Lord, without any contact with another individual.
3. What is the appropriate Biblical response when someone comes to you seeking your forgiveness?

Chapter 6

Why Is It So Hard to Forgive?

Years ago the Lord enabled me to adopt what I call my "up-front policy." Carrying bitterness, resentment, and unresolved conflicts had brought me to a state of hostility and bondage. I was tired of being lied to and taken advantage of. But confrontation was not my way; I didn't enjoy it at all! Why was I reluctant to approach others when offended? What was the real reason for my timidity?

"Only by pride cometh contention" (Prov. 13:10). I'll never forget the night God opened this verse to my heart and convicted me of the sin of pride. There was a growing distance between me and one of my closest friends. Those "little things" were piling up and putting a wedge between us. Differences had led to conflicts that had to be resolved if the friendship was to continue. God showed me that the contention between my friend and me was the result of pride—my pride!

First, I was afraid to confront my friend because I feared rejection. If I told him what I really thought, there was the possibility it would not be accepted. Would our friendship withstand total honesty? I wasn't sure. Since then I have learned that real friendship cannot be maintained apart from honesty and transparency. The possibility of losing a good friend posed an ominous threat to my pride. I feared rejection so I kept quiet.

Second, pride caused me to respond to my friend's faults and inconsistencies with a critical spirit instead of Godly concern. Pride eliminates compassion and institutes criticism instead. Critical and contentious attitudes indicate a root of pride. The only way to look down on someone is to assume you are better than they. A humble person recognizes he has faults and is capable of the worst, but a proud person sets himself up as judge and finds a multitude of reasons to condemn, many of which are true. The real problem is not recognizing the other man's faults but the way in which one responds to those faults. Instead of praying for my friend, it became increasingly easy to harbor resentment.

It has been said, "Where Satan can't go personally he just sends a critic!" The Bible refers to Satan as an "accuser" (Rev. 12:10). In the Garden of Eden he accused God of lying. *"And the serpent said unto the woman, Ye shall not surely die: For God doth know that in the day ye eat thereof, then your eyes shall be opened, and ye shall be as gods, knowing good and evil" (Genesis 3:4,5).* Here Satan contradicts what God said and accuses Him of concealing the truth from Adam and Eve. Satan not only slanders God, he also accuses man. Note Job 1:7-11:

> And the LORD said unto Satan, Whence comest thou? Then Satan answered the LORD, and said, From going to and fro in the earth, and from walking up and down in it. And the LORD said

unto Satan, Hast thou considered my servant Job, that there is none like him in the earth, a perfect and an upright man, one that feareth God and escheweth evil? Then Satan answered the LORD, and said, Doth Job fear God for nought? Hast not thou made an hedge about him, and about his house, and about all that he hath on every side? Thou hast blessed the work of his hands, and his substance is increased in the land. But put forth thine hand now, and touch all that he hath, and he will curse thee to thy face.

In Genesis he accused God to man; in Job he accuses man to God. How similar we are to Satan when we slander and criticize!

A compassionate soul will be broken, not bitter, over his brother's sins. Pride is the source of a critical, unforgiving spirit. The lack of concerned confrontation only intensifies the problem.

Third, my pride would not allow me to approach my friend because, if I did, it would expose my own needs. I did not want it known that such trivial matters really bothered me. If I got honest, my own weakness and wickedness would be unveiled. Pride will cost you friendships and a host of life's most valuable treasures. Pride can cause you to be quiet in order to save face rather than risk being laid bare by confronting the problem.

When the Holy Spirit showed me my pride, I knew the only way to crush it was to do the thing I feared the most. I had to go in lowliness and admit that the friction in our relationship was due to my pride. After I took the low road and acknowledged my faults, I was then able to share some honest concerns. This is what real friendships are made of—truthfulness. It was at this point I decided to be up-front all the time. When there is a misunderstanding or when you feel slighted, it is best to put your cards on the table. Approach the other party in calmness and truthfulness. Many times what seems obvious to one party is oblivious to the other. Get it resolved as soon as you can. Don't wait until your stomach is tied up in knots. Why not adopt your own "up-front policy" now?

There are other reasons for withholding forgiveness besides pride. One reason is selfishness. You have been hurt. You didn't deserve that unfair treatment. Things did not go as you had planned. By nature we all have a "god-complex." Somehow we believe we are entitled to preferential treatment. We think we have a right to be respected and treated well by all men. In fact, our selfishness is so intense that our primary concern is for our rights and our feelings. Once offended, we tend to live in an emotional prison because our expectations were not realized. Jesus invited His followers to take up the cross, which was an instrument of death, and follow Him. He asked them to die to their own way. Taking up the cross was a picture of surrendered rights and expectations. Do you need to surrender your rights to God?

Is it your own self-centeredness that is holding you back from making the right choices? You could choose to forgive, if you would. Perhaps you are willing to forgive if your offender would come and "confess up." You don't have to wait for an apology to forgive. When Stephen was being stoned he uttered a prayer on behalf of those who were stoning him: *"He kneeled down, and cried with a loud voice, Lord, lay not this sin to their charge" (Acts 7:60).* The Lord Jesus prayed, as he was hanging on the Cross, *"Father, forgive them; for they know not what they do" (Lk. 23:34).* Those wicked soldiers were not apologizing to the Lord. They were mocking Him. Yet, Jesus forgave and even asked His Father to forgive them. We are obligated to forgive regardless of what others do or don't do. There's no need to wait; go ahead and forgive. Pride and selfishness, two of Satan's main character traits, are two of the leading hindrances to forgiveness. Do you need to "take up the cross" and put to death this deadly duo?

Another hindrance to freedom is pain. Some experiences are so bad and hurt so much that many fear bringing up those painful emotions. This is especially true when there has been an attempt to bury them by denial or simply ignoring those memories.

One woman stood and said tearfully, "My father is ninety years old and is lying on his deathbed. When I was a little girl my father did terrible things to me. I just made a decision to forgive my father for all those horrible things he did to me." It was painful for this woman to face the things she had carried for over fifty years, but it was necessary. Incest, rape, child abuse, and the like are so unpleasant that people will run instead of deal with them. In such cases, healing may only come when there is a willingness to confront and work through forgiveness.

It was not easy for a young woman to forgive the man who raped her as a teenager. It was painful. Her conscience had been convicted. She knew she was obligated to forgive the man of his awful crime. With tears, trembling voice, and bent knee she prayed, "Lord, I am making a decision to forgive that man who took advantage of me as a teenager." As painful as this may be, it was the only way for her to recover from this life-shattering experience. Spiritual surgery may hurt, but it alone can bring about healing. Whatever scar it may leave will be easier to handle than the gaping wound you now bear.

In cases like these (incest and rape) the government is ordained by God to punish evildoers. Scripture teaches that civil authorities are to punish crimes such as these. In some groups there is a great misunderstanding of civil government's responsibility. *"For he is the minister of God to thee for good. But if thou do that which is evil, be afraid; for he beareth not the sword in vain: for he is the minister of God, a revenger to execute wrath upon him that doeth evil. Wherefore ye must needs be subject, not only for wrath, but also for conscience sake" (Rom. 13:4,5).* Never confuse our responsibility to forgive as Christians with the responsibility of the courts. When a crime has been committed we really do not have the right to pardon. That is the right of a court of law set up by God as His ministers for the purpose of avenging wrong. The government must punish the crime, but we as believers must forgive those who offend us. Justice is the duty of the judiciary; forgiveness is our part.

Questions for Personal Growth

Why Is It So Hard To Forgive?

1. List the three major reasons why forgiving is often very difficult. Which one(s) did God speak to you personally about?
2. What is the difference between "pardon" and "forgiveness"? Whose responsibility is each of these?

Chapter 7

What Do I Do When I'm Tempted to "Unforgive"?

Once you have made a choice to forgive, you must continue to choose the freedom of forgiveness. A decision to forgive is no guarantee that bitter thoughts and emotions will never return. It is only normal that deep wounds leave emotional scars. Don't think it strange when these thoughts and feelings arise; that's normal. Now you must learn to reverse your mental and conflicting emotional processes. Here are some helpful directives:

Rule #1. **Don't rehearse the details** once the case has been settled. One man, talking to another, said, "Every time my wife and I get in an argument, she gets historical." His friend said, "You mean **hysterical**?" "No," he said, "I mean **historical.** She brings up everything I've ever done, and just keeps bringing it back up." When you have chosen to forgive it will do you no good to rethink the circumstances and events. Dwelling on some aspect of the offense will only cause you to inwardly fume. Don't allow the Enemy to bombard you with recurring episodes of that same old story once you have closed the book!

These thoughts will return, but you must choose against mentally reviewing them. You do not have to allow a dwelling place to every thought that comes floating through your mind. Just as you decided to forgive, you must choose again and again not to review the story. Don't rehearse it!

Rule #2. **Don't nurse it.** "I really was taken advantage of." Hold everything! Now is not the time to have a pity party. Justifying yourself and building a case for your innocence is no longer needed. You have released the offending party from his debts. He owes you nothing. It's now between him and God. Do not take back a right to justice that you have given to God. As a Christian, your rights are surrendered anyway.

Sam Jones, an evangelist, had difficulty forgiving others of their wrongs to him, until one day he came to this: he said, "I thought of the grace of God and then made up my mind that I was not going to fall out with anybody until that person treated me worse than I had treated Jesus."

Yes, you were hurt, you were wronged, you were offended. But now that you have forgiven, you dare not indulge in feeling sorry for yourself. Don't nurse it!

Rule #3. **Don't curse it.** Vengeance is not ours; that belongs to God. Never allow any room for wicked thoughts of revenge toward the offender. "Well, he really deserves . . . ." Wait a minute! What he deserves is irrelevant. It's out of our hands. The Lord will do as He sees fit. It is not ours to wish or pray for evil on the person who has hurt us. Jesus said, *"Love your enemies, bless them that curse you, do good to them that hate you, and pray for them which despitefully use you..." (Matt. 5:44).* Notice: love, bless, do good, and pray. Herein lies the only way we can maintain a proper attitude. It was by an act of the will that forgiveness was granted. Likewise, by continual acts of love and prayer, we will be able to obtain and maintain a proper heart attitude.

Rule #4. **Do pray for them.** Here is the secret of staying free from bitterness. Do you remember Job? He was stripped of his possessions, children, and health, and then his three friends started accusing him and blaming him for all his troubles! They were confident that it was his sin that landed him in his awful plight. They were accusing him, and Job responded by praying for them! *"The LORD turned the captivity of Job, when he prayed for his friends..." (Job 42:10).* God released him from bondage when he prayed for his friends. They were not exactly the type of friends you feel like praying for. This is the secret of staying free.

Once two Christians embarked on a business agreement that initially was going to be beneficial for both. These men were friends as well as believers. One was a mechanic and he agreed to work on the other man's car. The man who owned the car lost a lot of money. He went to the mechanic, who refused to acknowledge his fault and wouldn't do anything to compensate. Immediately, a wall shot up between the men. The man with the car felt cheated. The whole episode went through his mind time and time again. He felt uncomfortable when he saw the other man. Anger would swell up every time they met. Although it was unnatural, the offended brother tried to be cordial because it was the Christian thing to do! Can you identify with this? We all can. What happened? The man who was taken advantage of decided to forgive his brother.

Even so, anger still arose. He tried his best to get free. Finally, he started praying for his friend and asked God to bless him. Every time the offense came to mind, he would pray. It didn't take long for the negative emotional response to disappear.

It is impossible to harbor resentment toward anyone when you pray for him or her consistently. Every time your anger toward an offender returns, immediately begin to pray for him. Ask God's blessing on him and his family. Believe me, you can't remain bitter while you're praying for someone. Every time those thoughts return, engage in prayer. In so doing, your attitudes and disposition will be transformed as you pray for those individuals. In time, your anger and emotional hostility will fade and be replaced by genuine love. Sometimes you may even find pity in your heart for the person who has hurt you. Making the right choices will keep you free from enslaving anger.

Yes, you can get along with everybody all the time! They may not get along with you, but you can do your part in getting along with them. When you respond properly to others, you are probably getting along with the Lord and at peace within yourself as well. Reconciliation, restitution, and forgiveness are God's way to deal with offenses. What steps must you take to reach the happy place where your heart and conscience are free?

Questions For Personal Growth

What Do I Do When I'm Tempted To "Unforgive"?

1. Is the following statement true or false? "Once I have forgiven an offender, the problem is over and I can rest assured it will never bother me again." Explain your answer.

2. List the four practical steps which can be taken to

avoid negative emotional responses once you have forgiven your offender(s). Purpose in your heart that you will observe them, asking God to remind you at those times when you are tempted to "unforgive."

Practical Steps to Forgiving Others

Here is a summary of what we've discussed in Section One. This is given to help you make thorough application by granting forgiveness to those who have offended you.

1. Understand that forgiveness is not :
   - Denying you were hurt
   - Forgetting or pushing painful experiences out of your mind
   - Initiating an emotion or feeling
   - Asking God to forgive you for being angry with the person who offended you
   - Asking God to pardon the person who hurt you
   - Justifying or understanding why your offender acted toward you as he or she did

2. Understand that forgiveness is:
   - A commandment and not a suggestion
   - Cancelling the debt and expecting nothing in return
   - A choice, an act of your will

3. Get alone with God and make a list of all the people who have offended you and the events for which you need to forgive them.

4. Ask God to forgive you for your bitterness toward your offenders.

5. Pray through your list out loud. Deal with each situation individually. Pray something like this, "Lord, I am choosing right now to forgive _____ for _____. I release them for hurting me and will never hold it against them again." Go through your entire list. When you're finished, tear up the "You-Owe-Me" list!

6. Thank the Lord for using this difficult situation to conform you to the image of His Son.

7. Understand that it is often unwise to inform the other party that you have forgiven them unless they have sought your forgiveness.

8. When bitter thoughts and hostile feelings return, immediately begin to pray for those who have hurt you.

Section 2

Seeking Forgiveness

Chapter 8

Is It Really Necessary to Ask Forgiveness?

Once you have forgiven others for their wrongs, you are ready to move on toward the second half of forgiveness. Forgiveness is to be granted, and it is to be sought. Believers are to seek forgiveness for their wrongs from both God and **man.** While this was touched on in the previous section, we need to see clearly our responsibility in obtaining a "clean slate."

First, you need to go to the Lord, if you haven't already, and confess your sins. Our relationship with God is affected by our many horizontal relationships. If we have sinned against people in unforgiveness, we have also sinned against the Lord. This needs to be confessed. The Bible states, *"If we confess our sins,* (agree with God about them) *he is faithful and just to forgive us our sins, and to cleanse us from all unrighteousness"* (*1 John 1:9).* That is the first step. Next, there may be the need to ask forgiveness and to make restitution.

"I'm not used to talking to you face to face; I normally talk behind your back. Will you forgive me?" This is what one woman tearfully said while standing in front of her fellow church members. Was this appropriate? In this case, yes. She had publicly sinned with her tongue by gossiping, and the entire church was aware of it. In this instance and many others, there is a need to seek forgiveness.

Let's examine those instances in which we have wronged another party. Once we are aware of an offense, we need to go to that person and seek reconciliation. The Holy Spirit's mission is conviction of sin. When the Spirit is brooding over an individual, he becomes aware of things previously unnoticed. A man who worked in a bakery was smitten with conviction about two bags of cookies he had stolen. Stealing was an automatic firing offense. So desperate was he to get a clear conscience that he went to his boss and confessed his sin. His employer was shocked; no one ever had come to him and admitted thievery and asked forgiveness. *(By the way, he didn't lose his job.)* A seminary president was surprised when a graduate returned his diploma and admitted cheating on an exam. In the middle of a church business meeting a man rose to his feet and said, "I was not wrong in what I said a moment ago, but I sure was wrong in the way I said it. Will you forgive me?" Can you imagine the IRS employee who opens an envelope and finds a check and letter admitting cheating the government? What do you think when a young man apologizes to his parents for his disrespect and rebellion? There is a common thread in all these cases: each individual is seeking to clear his conscience. A guilty conscience is unbearable. When God makes us aware of wrongs, we must respond in obedience.

Like a tall building, life's foundations must be deep, strong, and secure. Confession, forgiveness, and restitution are foundational principles for obedient, successful Christian living. Then comes the day-by-day, hour-by-hour, moment-by-moment task of appropriating these indispensable principles as needs arise. As long as you're on planet Earth you will need to apply God's rules for human relationships. These truths relate to the home, church, work, and neighborhood. By responding in total obedience, you can do your part in getting along with everybody all the time. This is the way to live!

Questions For Personal Growth

Is It Really Necessary To Ask Forgiveness?
1. Walking with God produces a sensitivity to offenses toward others which we commit. Spiritual dullness and insensitivity result from ignoring such offenses or failing to clear our consciences. Is there anyone who could face you at this moment and say, "You hurt me and never attempted to set things right"?
2. If there is such a person (or persons) purpose before God to obey Him as He directs you through the truths presented in this section of the book.

Chapter 9

But
What If . . . ?

A host of excuses may flood the soul of the one seeking forgiveness. Since this act of obedience is of such vital importance, it is not surprising that Satan would seek to cloud and confuse the issue. Excuses should be regarded squarely as satanic obstacles. Once convicted, the child of God must hurdle all obstacles hindering him from seeking forgiveness and recognize these warped reasonings for what they are: assaults of the Evil One. Do any of these sound familiar?

"It happened before I got saved." Once converted, our sins are forgiven, but that does not relieve us of the responsibility to make things right. Zacchaeus repaid all those whom he had cheated. His wrongs were prior to his conversion. A sign of genuine salvation is the desire to clear up wrongdoing. Once he had come to the Lord, Zacchaeus knew things needed to be put right.

You may be thinking, "I don't have enough years left to seek forgiveness from all the people I have wronged!" The Lord will point out those cases in which you need to act. Don't be overwhelmed. The thing you need to be concerned about now is your willingness to obey God in everything He reveals. God will guide along the way.

"I've lost track of them. They moved." One night a man stood in church and told of a most unusual answer to prayer he had received that day. When he was a teenager he worked at a service station where he stole money. This now middle-aged man told the Lord he would put this right if he ever saw his old boss. The service station owner had moved, and he had not seen him for years. Guess who he saw at the bank the very day after he prayed? The service station owner! What a glowing testimony he gave that night.

When the attempt to locate an offended party fails, there is a way to clear the matter. A lady had stolen from the department store where she worked while attending high school. The store had closed, and she didn't have any idea where the owner lived. I counseled her to pray about it and tell the Lord she was willing to put it right if their paths ever crossed. Meanwhile, I suggested she give an equivalent sum to her church. Having done all in her power to pay back the stolen money, she could honestly say she had sought forgiveness. She did not have to feel guilty about it any more.

"It was so small." If it's big enough to bother you, it's a good sign it needs to be dealt with. Things taken from the office, half-truths that were told, unChrist-like responses and the other "small" things need to be acted on. In taking care of the small things, you narrow the likelihood of overlooking the larger things. Wrong is wrong, whether large or small.

"I'm too sensitive." Better to be too sensitive than calloused with a seared conscience. If you really are too sensitive, the Lord can moderate that problem. But

violating your conscience through disobedience is a serious matter. Hardening your conscience will render you unable to hear God's voice, and larger problems can be rationalized, excused, and overlooked.

"I can't afford it; money is involved." Picture this scenario: a Canadian couple is sitting in the pastor's office. The man is terribly distressed, and the wife is fearful her husband is going to get "too honest." The man breaks down and pours out his soul. He tells how he and his wife had purchased camera equipment in the U.S. and brought it back into Canada without paying tax on it. The pastor phones the border agency and explains the situation. The wife is weeping, fearing her husband will go to jail. The border agent tells them simply to bring in the tax money. Because of fear, this dear woman had complicated what turned out to be a simple situation. The Lord knows about your finances. He can supply your needs. Don't allow this excuse to side-track your obedience to God.

"They will not understand." You may be surprised how much they will understand. Most people are so taken back by honesty that they not only understand, they also gladly forgive. In the vast majority of cases I know about, there has been a positive response.

But remember, their response is not the most important thing. There is no guarantee the other party will react positively. You are out to obey God by clearing your conscience. All God asks is that you obey. Whether they receive it or not is between them and God. Once you do your part, you are free! The most important thing is total obedience on your part.

Questions For Personal Growth

But What If . . . ?

1. Someone has suggested that an excuse is "the skin of a reason stuffed with a lie." Satan is the father of lies and will do all in his power to thwart or delay obedience in this crucial matter of clearing the conscience. Take a moment to list the six excuses detailed in this chapter. Are you using any of these excuses as a means to avoid obeying God in seeking forgiveness? Reject any such excuses and seek God's grace to obey Him fully.

2. What might be done if you are unable, after prayer, to locate a party to whom you need to make restitution?

3. If there is a situation involving the need to make restitution concerning money, use a concordance and seek to locate passages of Scripture which might give principles concerning proper repayment. These can be found in both Old and New Testaments. Determine before God what He would have you do in the particular case and trust Him to enable you to do it.

Chapter 10

How Can I Tell If My Conscience Is Violated?

The numerous New Testament references to conscience indicate its importance. Once the conscience is offended, serious repercussions result. See if you can identify with any of these signs that indicate a violated conscience.

Uncontrollable anger. When certain people or subjects are discussed, you tend to strike out in anger. You "can't stand" to be around certain people. When you meet them in the grocery store you'll go out of your way to avoid them. It is easy to by-pass the gas station or post office when you spot their car. And if you accidently find yourself in their presence your pulse accelerates. You can't explain it, but you are not able to control your feelings. Inwardly you are about to explode. You know they sense your frustration. The longer you stay in their presence the more the tension mounts.

Anxiety. Are you overly nervous and irritable? Has the

gentle dove, the Holy Spirit, taken His flight from controlling your soul? *"Let the peace of God rule in your heart" (Col. 3:15)*. Part of the fruit of the Holy Spirit is peace. When we are controlled by the Spirit, we have peace in our souls. Picture the role of the Spirit as a referee in your heart. When a foul (sin) has been committed, the referee blows the whistle. You lose your peace. The Bible promises a peace that is beyond comprehending. Anxiety and nervousness may be due to a number of reasons, and one is an unclear conscience.

Critical Mindset. We are not called upon to act as a spiritual gestapo. It is not our place to preside as judge over mankind. Of course, we are called to judge righteous judgment, but that is very different from a judgmental, hyper-critical attitude. Criticism often is a defense mechanism with which men justify themselves. When distrust, suspicion, and cynicism become an obsession, it is a sure sign of a deeper problem. If you are proficient at fault-finding and analytical indictments come easily, then carefully consider this verse: *"Therefore thou art inexcusable, O man, whosoever thou art that judgest: for wherein thou judgest another, thou condemnest thyself; for thou that judgest doest the same things" (Rom. 2:1)*.

Have you noticed that the things that bother you about other people are generally the things you are guilty of yourself? How much easier to condemn another than to admit I'm in the same boat! When you're critical, you can't love your friends, much less your enemies. Such is the bitter fruit of a violated conscience.

Lack of love. Are you able to articulate a detailed catalog of hurts? Is this list contrary to the characteristics of love found in 1 Corinthians 13? Charity (love) is kind, envies not, is not puffed up, not easily provoked, thinks no evil, beareth all things, rejoices not in evil, hopes all things, and endures all things. Do you lack love? Do you have an attitude problem?

God is love. This is the chief fruit of the Spirit. Love is the greatest motivator in the world. When God's love is shed abroad in our hearts, we are granted supernatural ability to feel and show concern. The absence of love is proof that the Spirit has been grieved.

We are called to be as Jesus, broken bread and poured out wine. Our position is that of servants, love-slaves of Jesus Christ. When compassion is not present, something serious is amiss.

Guilt. Do you struggle with guilt over things in your past? Does this tend to preoccupy your mind and make you unable to concentrate? Are you forever preaching to yourself, "If only I had never done . . ."? Are you tormented by plaguing thoughts of regret?

Guilt is God's means to bring us to a place of repentance, humility, and brokenness. As we have seen, the blood of Jesus cleanses the guilty sinner. With Calvary and the brokenness of Jesus in view, we are compelled to appeal there for mercy and enabled to make amends with our fellow man. Once we see the brokenness of the Creator for our sin, it is only right to be broken because of our sin. Brokenness is a necessary prerequisite for restitution.

Joylessness. Do you often find yourself depressed and fatigued? Has your zest for life dissipated? Have you lost the joy of your salvation? When the cup of joy isn't overflowing there is a leak in the cup! Nothing drains energy and depletes joy faster than a soiled conscience.

Like love and peace, joy also is a fruit of the Spirit. Inner joy, cups running over, is a tremendous benefit of life in Christ! The pathway to freedom is forgiveness and restoration.

Self-Condemnation. Belittling ourselves is neither

healthy nor helpful. When the conscience is guilty, how easy it is to take a stick to ourselves. Self-induced floggings, whether verbal or merely mental, will complicate the dilemma. Some mistake self-criticism for humility. In reality, it is the exact opposite—pride. Pride does not always manifest itself as haughtiness; sometimes it disguises itself in mock-humility. Self-condemnation is the opposite of true brokenness. God wants obedience, not self-degradation. Evading responsibility is but another tactic to by-pass responsibility to God and man.

Abnormal fears. One man told me he had such a fear of heights that he was scared to go up to the second floor in a building. That's totally unnatural. Fear is sometimes a by-product of a guilty conscience. *"God has not given us the spirit of fear; but of power, and of love, and of a sound mind" (2 Tim. 1:7).* How many fears are really just complications from inner guilt? *"Perfect love casts out fear" (1 Jn. 4:18).* Love is demonstrated through obedience. *"If you love me,"* Jesus said, *"keep my commandments" (John 14:15).* Often these inordinate fears vanish when the conscience is cleared by obedience.

Externals and activity. In order to placate a guilty conscience, some overemphasize external conformity and religious activity. To compensate for the past a high standard is set, be it external conformity, or great pride in abstaining from certain practices. Jesus spoke of the Pharisees who were clean outwardly but defiled inwardly. Strict adherence to self-imposed codes and constant activity, while neglecting other priorities, can be a substitute for genuine restoration.

Isolation. The man concealing a bad conscience cannot afford to allow others to get too close. There's always the danger of being found out. A small circle of friends kept at a distance minimizes the chances of exposure. Without brokenness there can be no openness, and without openness there will be no oneness.

Defensiveness. Only the teachable can be taught. Only the approachable can be approached. Proverbs speaks of the wise who will benefit from corrective rebukes while fools despise instruction. It is possible to rationalize and justify just about anything. *"All the ways of a man are clean in his own eyes; but the LORD weigheth the spirits" (Prov. 16:2).* Defensive roadblocks, rather than protecting, obstruct the true healing which can only come through reconciliation.

Questions For Personal Growth

How Can I Tell If My Conscience Is Violated?

1. Skim through the list of indicators of a defiled conscience given in the chapter. Which one(s) apply to you? Make a note of them.
2. Ask the Lord to search your heart for the offenses you have committed that have produced these symptoms. List those whom you have offended. Take appropriate steps to clear your conscience after completing item 3 below.
3. As a Bible study, go through the Beatitudes (Matthew 5:3-12) and relate each of the eleven indicators of a violated conscience to one or more of the attitudes reflected in the Beatitudes. Clearing the conscience requires not only going, but going in the right spirit or attitude. Which Godly attitudes need to be cultivated in your life as you prepare to clear your conscience?

Chapter 11

How Do I Cleanse My Conscience?

Many adverse results can be avoided by living in obedience to God's Word. When it comes to a clear conscience there is only one way to be happy in Jesus, and that is to trust and obey.

The conscience is an inward monitor that gauges our inclinations and actions. The purpose of conscience is to correct and reprimand us when we do wrong or when we are about to do wrong. It is a very delicate instrument and when working correctly it is sensitively tuned, but not over sensitive. The conscience functions as an inner alarm, forewarning us of potential danger. There is no alternative to a clear conscience. Hard work, excellent knowledge, or strong emotions will not substitute for a conscience which is fine-tuned by the Holy Spirit and the Holy Word.

Some have described it as the window of the soul. Dirt, dust, and smut will hinder light from passing through a window. A sufficient coat of filth will totally block out the light. The conscience is a window through which God's light shines to expose our fault. When we submit to its voice and eliminate the sin it condemns, the strength and clarity of conscience is reinforced. The light shines brighter next time. But when we don't obediently respond to the inner voice, our conscience becomes hardened (desensitized); sin accumulates. The window is clouded and the light barely penetrates. The conscience can become seared (1 Tim. 4:2) or paralyzed. In this state there is no grief for sin, only a dull insensitivity to the voice of God. This spells serious trouble!

Christianity is a religion of the conscience. It is more than adherence to externals; it is a heart in tune with God. Once we are convicted that a wrong needs to be put right, we must obey or violate our conscience. Titus 1:5 refers to a defiled conscience. When there is defilement in the conscience it acts like a faulty thermostat; it doesn't respond at the right time! It is off-beat, out of step with where it should be. The Bible speaks of a "good conscience" (1 Pet. 3:16; 1 Tim. 1:9). Paul said, *"Herein do I exercise myself, to have always a conscience void of offense toward God, and toward men" (Acts 24:16).* But how do we obtain a good conscience that is void of offense?

The clearing of the conscience is two-fold: toward God and man. Old Testament sacrifices and ceremonies were insufficient to cleanse the conscience (Heb. 9: 9; 10:1-2). So, in the course of time God sent His Son. *"For if the blood of bulls and of goats, and the ashes of a heifer sprinkling the unclean, sanctifieth to the purifying of the flesh: How much more shall the blood of Christ, who through the eternal Spirit offered himself without spot to God, **purge your conscience** from dead works to serve the living God?" (Heb. 9:13-14).*

So powerful is the blood of Jesus that it gives us good standing in God's sight and bids us come boldly into the holiest (Hebrews 10:19). Our guilt, our sins, and everything in us which is opposed to God was dealt with on the Cross. The forgiveness of sins is not only judicial, but is also experiential. In other words, the cleansing by Christ's blood is so deep that it is to be felt by the forgiven sinner. No wonder we are challenged to *"draw near in . . . full assurance of faith, having our hearts sprinkled from an evil conscience" (Heb. 10:22).* On a practical level, how does this happen?

"But if we walk in the light, as he is in the light, we have fellowship one with another, and the blood of Jesus Christ his Son cleanseth us from all sin. If we confess our sins, he is faithful and just to forgive us our sins, and to cleanse us from all unrighteousness" (1 Jn. 1:7,9).

Walking in the light is simply a willingness to get out in the open. When the light exposes the darkness in our lives, immediately we are to confess and forsake it. There can be no hiding, denying, or rationalizing. We must agree with God about sin. Simply put, the way to walk in the light is to keep the window of conscience clean by responding immediately and completely to its voice. Forgiveness comes through confession. Cleansing comes through walking in the light because as we walk in light the blood of Jesus Christ cleanses us from all sin. When you walk in the light you never walk alone, for the Scripture says, *"we have fellowship one with another."*

The conscience is made faultless before God by the blood of Christ. If our conscience is clear toward man it is because we have acted obediently in seeking forgiveness. Zacchaeus, after his conversion, paid back everyone he had cheated. Remember Jesus' words, "first be reconciled." The matter of a good conscience is invaluable. First Timothy 1:5 states, *"The end of the commandment is . . . a good conscience."* The purpose or goal of God's Word is to bring about a clear conscience. That means I must settle the "I-owe-you" list.

In Bible times the towns and villages likely had a silversmith in residence. This silversmith had a shop and a large pot for melting metal. The metal ore would be placed in the pot with an extremely hot fire beneath it, hot enough to melt the ore. Once liquefied the impurities would float to the top and the smith would skim off the scum. The metal would cool and harden. Then a hotter fire would be built beneath the ore and the hotter temperatures would cause a different type of impurity to surface. This process, repeated with more intense heat each time, would bring a different type of impurity to the surface. In each case the metal smith would skim off the impurities.

The Lord uses the heat caused by the friction of human relationships to cause our impurities to surface. People don't create impurities within us, but they can cause them to surface. Someone said, "If you want to know what you are full of, see what spills out when you're jostled." No one can make you hate; nevertheless, some can bring out hidden problems. The heat doesn't cause the scum; it merely exposes what's inside. Suppose the metal ore was liquefied and an awful scum had surfaced. Unless the smith ladled it off, it would sink back into the metal as it cooled. It would not even be seen until the heat was reapplied and then it would reappear. When scum arises it must be dealt with. Nobody likes dealing with the scum, but it is absolutely necessary.

When relationships heat up—in the home, church, or business—and impurities are exposed, we have several choices. First, we can run from the fire, but that only brings temporary relief. When things heat up in marriage, many will abandon their commitment and marry someone else. Initially, the angry emotions subside as things cool down. But it won't take long before friction brings forth heat and the scum on the inside will resurface. Running from the problem, getting out of the fire will never solve anything. It merely allows impurities to submerge and settle down where they're undetected, but the impurities are still there. God's way is not to avoid relationships, but to learn the proper response in each situation.

Secondly, we can deal with the defilement. Changing churches every time something occurs is not the answer. Examples from Scripture indicate that God is more concerned about our response than what actually happens to us. There will be offenses. People will offend us and their offenses can bring out ugly attitudes and actions from inside us. Thorough cleansing calls for thorough dealing with the scum. It's messy, but it's the only way to be cleansed.

The pressure from dealing with others is God's way of purifying His people. It is a process. The silversmith heats and skims, then heats it hotter and skims again until that liquid silver is so pure that he can look at it and see the reflection of his face. This is what God is doing with us. He wants us so holy that as He looks at us He can see His own image! Oh, the blessing of a conscience void of offense toward God and man.

Questions For Personal Growth

How Do I Cleanse My Conscience?
1. What is the purpose of the conscience?
2. In what significant way does Christianity differ from other "religions" regarding the conscience?
3. The Christian is sent into spiritual warfare with only two major weapons: faith and a good conscience (1 Timothy 1:19). How is such a conscience gained and maintained?

4. Describe a major purpose of God in our lives through relationships with others and the hurts they bring.

Chapter 12

What About Repentance?

When a person is truly forgiven, does it show? Most of us have seen the popular bumper-sticker that reads, "Christians Aren't Perfect . . . Just Forgiven!" Reactions to this message may vary according to our perspective. If you're traveling down a crowded highway and someone with that bumper-sticker suddenly cuts you off, endangering your life and the lives of others, you likely see the bumper-sticker as an excuse to justify hazardous driving. Should you see that car coming again another day, you might see it as a warning: Steer clear of those forgiven Christians—they can kill you! If you become incensed by this traffic hazard and are tempted to say or do something in return, you may view the message of the bumper-sticker as a rationale for your own feelings, and if you go ahead with your revenge, the message again becomes an excuse for wrong behavior. It all depends on perspective.

Scripture indicates that it is more than just perspective. Note the message of John the Baptist in Matthew 3. *"In those days came John the Baptist, preaching in the wil-*

derness of Judaea, And saying, Repent ye: for the kingdom of heaven is at hand . . . Bring forth therefore fruits meet for repentance"(verses 1-2, 8).* This indicates that true repentance shows in a person's life. And this truth is not limited to the Old Testament or pre-Calvary era. Paul, the apostle of grace, testified before King Agrippa in Acts 26:19-20 with these words: *"Whereupon, O king Agrippa, I was not disobedient unto the heavenly vision: But shewed first unto them of Damascus, and at Jerusalem, and throughout all the coasts of Judaea, and then to the Gentiles, that they should repent and turn to God, **and do works meet for repentance.**"* True repentance manifests itself in changed behavior and changed attitudes. People have every right to form an opinion about the genuineness of our forgiveness by the manner in which we drive if we have a "Christians aren't perfect . . . just forgiven" bumper-sticker. When we are truly repentant, and truly forgiven, it shows! People will judge the sincerity of our asking forgiveness from them by whether we communicate a spirit of repentance.

When we have offended, sinned against, or wronged another individual, genuine repentance is the key if we would seek their forgiveness. The word "repent" is a very unpopular word in our modern society. Yet, it is a very popular word in Scripture, appearing more than 950 times! God takes it very seriously. Sadly, repentance, whether toward God or men, is a much misunderstood and underused concept. It is all but missing today. What then is repentance?

More Than Conviction

First, **repentance goes beyond being convicted we are wrong.** It is possible to know beyond doubt that we are wrong, but do nothing about it. Every Gospel preacher has seen people touched by God through the preaching of His Word to the point that their knuckles turn white from gripping the pew. Like Felix in confrontation with Paul, they desire a "convenient season" in which to repent. Genuine repentance is much more than having a finger put on the problem and knowing we are wrong.

More Than Confession

Perhaps you are thinking now, "Yes, I not only need to be convicted that I am wrong, but I need to go to the one I have hurt and confess my wrong." While this is true, we must realize that **repentance also goes beyond confession of wrong.** Real repentance involves more than admitting, "I have sinned, I was wrong." Scripture records the plain confessions of at least five men who stated categorically, "I have sinned." Yet, none of these five exhibited true repentance.

When faced with multiplying plagues, Pharaoh confessed, "*I have sinned. God is righteous. I and the people are wicked.*" (Exodus 9:22-27). What more could we want? Verse 34 of the same chapter tells the full story: "*...when Pharaoh saw that the rain and the hail and the thunders were ceased, he sinned yet more, and hardened his heart, he and his servants.*" The conviction and confession born in the storm died in the calm! Pharaoh simply wasn't real in his repentance. Confessing merely because we are in a hard spot and do not like the consequences our actions have brought upon us is not sufficient.

Balaam is another example. Balaam was a prophet of sorts, but one who was greedy. He got caught and so he confessed, "*I have sinned*" (Numbers 22:34). He pretended that he didn't know what he was doing. Balaam wanted to serve God but rake in some extra profits. He got caught and made a hypocritical confession. See the rest of his "confession": "*. . . Lord, I have sinned . . . now therefore, if it displease thee, I will get me back again*" (Numbers 22:34). How many Balaamites there are today! They piously confess one day, but the next day there is no difference.

King Saul in 1 Samuel 15:24 made a wonderful-sounding confession. He clearly admitted that he had sinned and transgressed the commandment of God. Had he stopped there, he may have been moving in the right direction. But he then offered an alibi, attempting to pass the blame and justify himself. His was only a half-hearted confession. He didn't mean business at all.

In like fashion, Achan in the Old Testament and Judas Iscariot in the New confessed their sin, but not in genuine repentance. Without repentance, confession becomes as phony as a letter dated February 31!

More Than Contrition

If repentance is not just knowing we are wrong, not just confessing that we are wrong, then it must be that we must feel sorry for our wrong. While more weeping and tears over sin and wrong are certainly in order, even this is not synonymous with authentic repentance. Shedding rivers of crocodile tears does not prove there has been repentance. **Repentance goes beyond contrition over wrong.** Tears may lead to repentance, but tears and sorrow alone do not constitute actual repentance.

While conviction of wrong, confession of wrong, and contrition over wrong are steps to repentance, what composes real repentance?

Heart Change

Repentance first involves a change of heart. This simply means turning and going in a different direction. It is turning our back on something, be it an attitude or activity. It is not tipping our hat to something. It involves an unfeigned, inward change.

Perhaps you are familiar with the story of the man who for years had come forward in almost every special church meeting and prayed in a loud voice, "Lord, please clean the cobwebs out of my heart." This he prayed so many times with no evidence of any change in his life, that finally one brother, upon hearing the prayer once more, rose to his feet and cried out, "Forget those cobwebs, Lord; just kill that spider!" "Killing the spider," if you please, is what repentance is about.

A Whole-Heart Change

If a beautiful bride and her husband-to-be stood in front of the preacher and in response to the question, "Will you be faithful to your wife?" the wishful groom replied, "Well, I'll be 80% faithful," it is likely she would have second thoughts about the marriage. Repentance is not an 80% turn. It's not an 80% change. **Repentance involves a whole-heart change.** Repentance involves deep commitment. It is never a light thing.

A Continual Heart Change

Thirdly, **repentance is a continual heart change.** Repentance involves a commitment that is lived out on a daily basis. It begins at a point in time, yes, but it has continuing effect. The simple fact is, unless there is definitive, lasting change in the life of a person, there has been no repentance. When we repent, there is a difference. When others see that difference—the fruits that are suited to repentance—then they will believe our confession of wrong and be more likely to grant our request for forgiveness.

Fruits of Repentance

There are certain attitudes that accompany bona-fide repentance, attitudes that demonstrate a complete change of heart that has permanent impact. One of these is a demonstration of love, affection, and appreciation. One who is repentant in spirit has an inner awareness of how much God has forgiven him and the enormous cost required for that to occur. He is overwhelmed with the forgiveness he has in Christ.

When the woman of poor reputation crashed the dinner party at Simon's house and lavished the bottle of expensive ointment on the Lord Jesus, washing his feet with her tears and wiping them dry with her "glory," her hair, there was a demonstration of gratitude for forgiveness. She had been forgiven much and she loved much. Martin Luther referred to this woman's tears as "heart water." Her tears expressed what was going on in her heart in terms of love and gratefulness. **Repentant, forgiven people love more**.

There are two types of sorrow. One expresses sadness over what one has lost. The other expresses sadness over what one has done. One type leads to despair and depression. The other leads to repentance. The classic illustration of this in the Bible is the story of the prodigal in Luke 15. His was not merely a sorrow over the horrible consequences he had brought upon himself, not a sorrow that life had finally caught up with him, but a Godly sorrow that brought him to his senses. Have you ever noted from the story that the possibility of an immediate and complete restoration had never entered the prodigal's mind? He doesn't dream of being restored to his previous position. He thirsts only for forgiveness. He offers no alibis, no justifications. He might have pointed out some lack in his home life, the severity of the famine he experienced, his self-righteous brother, or some other circumstance. He made no attempt to re-tell the story and make himself appear the victim of someone else's problem. He was broken over his own wrong. He begged for mercy and forgiveness. Repentance makes us willing to beg the one we have offended for merciful forgiving. **Repentant people demonstrate humility, not presumption.** Repentant and forgiven people demand less.

Forgiven, repentant individuals love more, demand less, and **are quick to forgive others when they recognize true repentance.** The Lord Jesus said in Luke 17:3, "...*If thy brother trespass against thee, rebuke him; and if he repent, forgive him.*" The French commentator Godet wrote, "*Holiness and love meet in this precept: Holiness demands repentance; love forgives quickly and often.*" The fourth verse of Luke 17 says love will forgive seven times in one day if necessary. A similar passage in Matthew indicates seventy times seven.

God gives us the responsibility to evaluate our attitude and determine if our repentance is real or not. And he also makes us responsible to take risks and forgive. True repentance takes place in the heart. It is never superficial, it is never just words. True forgiveness is the same way.

How do we discern repentance? If you are looking for real repentance, examine love. Forgiven people, repentant people love more. Not just in sentimentality, but in endurance, kindness, thinking the best of others, wanting what's best for others, keeping a pure tongue, exhibiting patience with those who may have a hard time forgiving them.

Forgiven people, people where real repentance has taken place are not demanding. They are humble. They realize they don't deserve it. They wait for God to bring good things back into their lives.

It also takes time for fruit to show. One doesn't purchase

an apple tree, stick it in the ground, and stand there waiting for his apples. It takes time for the fruits of repentance to be fully ripe, but it doesn't take forever. Those who are repentant will focus on demonstrating fruit rather than demanding acceptance and confidence from others. When you are truly repentant, it shows!

Questions For Personal Growth

What About Repentance?

1. In seeking forgiveness, an attitude of repentance is vital. Briefly define genuine repentance, both negatively and positively, based on your understanding of this chapter.

2. When repentance is genuine, certain characteristics will be evident in the life. List these and evaluate your own repentance, first toward God, and then toward anyone you have wronged.

Chapter 13

How Do I Ask Forgiveness ?

Now comes the all-important matter of acting on what you know you must do. Don't rush recklessly into things without first mapping out a Scriptural path. The Bible gives clear directions for seeking forgiveness. God must prepare the way. In many situations there is no question about immediate action. In other cases, the Lord must initiate. Be willing to obey God as He opens the door. Pray right now, "Lord, I am personally willing to make restitution just as soon as the way is prepared." When the Lord initiates, act immediately. In some situations it is important that the other party is ready to receive you. God will make it clear as you are in tune with Him. At times the reception may not be to your liking, but when you move in God's timing, it will be the way He planned and bring about His desired results.

You must tear up the list of "You-Owe-Me's" when granting forgiveness, but when seeking forgiveness you must make a list of "I-Owe-You's." List the people you have hurt and the nature of your offense. Chances are you already have such a list, and your conscience is forever bringing it up! Ask God if there are other situations that require attention. God will show you exactly those instances that you need to act on.

When it comes to asking forgiveness, it is always one-sided. Never look to the other person to take, even share, the blame. Seeking forgiveness deals only with my guilt in a given matter. As far as I am concerned, it is my sole responsibility to make things right because I am dealing only with my wrongs.

The scope of your confession will be determined by the scope of your transgression. Personal sin should be confessed to God. Private sins should be dealt with among those involved. Public sin calls for public confession. Reconciliation should be governed by these guidelines.

Next, you must go to the offended party. Remember, Jesus said, *"Leave there thy gift before the altar, and go thy way; first* (you) *be reconciled" (Matt. 5:24).* Once God has spoken and you know what to do, don't wait for that person to come to you; you must go to him. Be very clear in your choice of wording. Say something like this: "I am sorry for (name your offense). I was wrong. Will you forgive me?" Should the other party deny you wronged him or should he attempt to dismiss the matter, press him again with, "God has convicted me. I was wrong. I am sorry. Will you forgive me?" Once you have obeyed God, you are free, no matter how he responds.

Never say, "If I offended you, I am sorry." Never stand before a congregation and say, "If I've ever hurt anyone here, please forgive me." Deal with the certainties. The "ifs" never resolve anything. If restitution deals with my blame, then it must be that I have offended, hurt, or allowed wrong attitudes to remain in my mind.

In matters of immorality there is no need to go into

detail. Rehearsing illicit episodes is not a healthy practice. The Scriptures say it is a shame even to speak of such things (Ephesians 5:12). A telephone call may be the best way to handle such cases. It is dangerous to put things on paper because you never know who will read it. A written confession also provides a continual reminder of your offense, which may only deepen bitter feelings. Renewing acquaintances may unwisely rekindle emotions. Caution must be exercised. If possible, call the offended party, and get right to the point. Ask forgiveness for wrongs. There should be no need for lengthy conversation. Say what you must in order to clear your conscience.

In cases of dishonesty and stealing, amends need to be made. You should return the merchandise, pay for what you've taken, or offer a plan for repayment. Zacchaeus, after his conversion, paid back four times as much as he had taken. The Bible does not demand this, but there needs to be just restitution.

Consult your pastor or spiritual leader if you are in doubt. *"In the multitude of counsellors there is safety" (Prov. 11:14).* Godly counsel from mature believers may be necessary. Some cases are so delicate that great wisdom is needed. Don't hesitate to seek help from a third party.

These Scriptural guidelines on granting and seeking forgiveness are essential for fruitful living as Christians. Forgiveness lies at the base of our life in Christ. The Lord Jesus bore our punishment so God's justice could be satisfied and sinners like us could be pardoned. Since we are forgiven, we now must forgive others who have wronged us and seek forgiveness from those we have wronged—for Christ's sake. By humbling ourselves before God and man, we can live free from guilt with deep inward peace. Don't let pride stand in the way. Obey God no matter the cost . *"To obey is better than sacrifice"* *(1 Sam. 15:22).*

Questions For Personal Growth

How Do I Ask For Forgiveness?

1. After prayerfully committing yourself to obedience to God in seeking forgiveness, write out your "I-Owe-You" list as mentioned in this chapter. Top the list with those you have hurt the most.

2. Which of God's commands did you violate in committing each offense? List them beside the individual's names.

3. Seek God first in repentance for your sins toward Him and His Holy Word.

4. What determines the scope or extent of your confession to others in seeking forgiveness?

5. Go to the individual from whom you need to ask forgiveness after working out a specific statement of your wrong toward them. Follow the guidelines given in the chapter.

6. What was the response of each person on your "I-Owe-You" list? Commit to God any who may not have responded positively. Thank Him for the grace to obey.

Practical Steps When Seeking Forgiveness

This is a capsule of the things we've talked about in Section Two. Follow these guidelines when seeking forgiveness from those you have offended.

1. Make a list of the people you have wronged. Ask God to bring to your remembrance every situation that needs to be acted on. Compile your "I-Owe-You" list.

2. Go to God and confess your offenses as sin. Agree with God about each situation. Thank God for His forgiveness.

3. Tell the Lord you are willing to go to the people on your list. Now you are ready to go and put things right. Some situations call for God's timing and you may need to ask God to prepare their hearts. If you are in doubt, consult with your pastor or spiritual advisor.

4. Asking forgiveness is always one-sided as far as you're concerned. Never ask the other person to share the blame.

5. Confess personal sin to God. Private sin should be acknowledged to those involved. Public sin calls for public confession. The scope of your confession is determined by the scope of your transgression.

6. Use clear wording and get to the point. "I was wrong in _____. I am sorry. Will you forgive me?"

7. When restitution needs to be made, as in cases of stealing, make appropriate amends.

8. Don't hesitate to consult your pastor if you are unclear in how to proceed.

9. Act in obedience! Do what you know you need to do. It may be difficult at first, but after you start it will seem like weights being removed from your shoulders. **It will be a blessing!**

10. Don't let the Enemy talk you out of obtaining God's blessing by total obedience.

Section 3

Enjoying Forgiveness

Chapter 14

What Are The Contagious Fruits of Forgiving?

The Bible commentator William Arnot relates the story of a traveler in Burma who crossed a river and quickly found his entire body covered by a host of leeches. As the leeches busily sucked out his blood, his first reaction was to tear the tormenting creatures from his flesh. But his servant warned him that to do so would place his very life in peril. Tearing them off would leave parts which would become seriously infected. The leeches, he was told, would have to drop off spontaneously to be rendered harmless. The servant prepared his master an herbal bath in which the master was told to lie. When he had bathed in the balsam, the leeches dropped off. Arnot applied the story with these words:

> Each unforgiven injury rankling in the heart is like a leech sucking the life-blood. Mere human deter-

mination to have done with it will not cast the evil thing away. You must bathe your whole being in God's pardoning mercy; and these venomous creatures will instantly let go their hold. You will stand up free.[1]

What a marvelous freedom and relief is found in forgiving! It is a joy which wells up within the depths of the soul, overflowing to all around us. It is a joy that cannot be contained; the results are infectious. To forgive is to tap the riches of God. Corrie ten Boom, the lovely lady whose family hid Jews in their home in Holland during the reign of Hitler, knew deeply the joy and fruit of forgiving. Arrested by the Nazis and sent to concentration camps, she alone of her family survived the war. Despite the deaths of all her loved ones and the unspeakable treatment they all received at the hands of the Nazis, Corrie refused to hate. She forgave. And as a result God gave her a worldwide ministry which has touched and continues to touch the hearts of millions.

Reconciliation

"I have forgiven that person who offended me, but I would rather not be around them." Does that sound like forgiveness? "I have forgiven my husband, but I'm not going to go back to him." Do such people really want reconciliation or merely the easing of their consciences? Genuine forgiveness makes friends out of enemies. Peace replaces hostility. Just as God forgives and reconciles the erring sinner, it is our purpose to reconcile those whom we have forgiven. Our calling is to build bridges, not walls. Nothing gives a parent greater joy than to see his children love one another. And our Heavenly Father derives great joy from seeing us love each other. The great truth of the Deity of Christ is seen in the oneness of God's people. Our

Lord prayed in His High Priestly prayer in John 17, *"that they may be one, that the world might believe that Thou hast sent Me."* Ours is to restore, not alienate. This may not be easy, but is essential.

Matthew 18:15 says, *"Moreover, if thy brother shall trespass against thee, go and tell him his fault between thee and him alone; if he shall hear thee, thou hast gained thy brother."* How wonderful! A brother or sister has been gained! What a precious thing it is when brethren are reconciled. There are no problems too big to solve, only people too small to solve them. How many devastated marriages could be saved if those involved were willing to forgive and work through to reconciliation? How much unity of love and fellowship could families enjoy if family members would forgive and be reconciled one to another? What multitudes of children could be spared from delinquency if Mom and Dad would be reconciled? How much more blessing would churches know if members were willing to forgive and be reconciled? Reconciliation is one of the contagious results of forgiving.

Revival

Following hard on the heels of reconciliation is revival. Revival is simply getting right with God and right with one another. Unforgiveness is one of the major barricades to revival in our churches. D. L. Moody said, "The one sin that is doing more to hold back the power of God in revival than any other sin is an unforgiving spirit."

Miss Bertha Smith, veteran missionary during the great Shantung revival in China, testified that revival began when the missionaries were convicted of unforgiving spirits and began to confess their sins one to another and to forgive one another.

Small, petty things can quickly become bitterness and

wreak havoc. Scripture warns it is *"the little foxes that spoil the vines."* Soon, the power of God's Holy Spirit is shut out from a congregation. But as people begin to confess and forgive, God once again moves in power.

Someone has said that revival is not just getting the roof off, but it is also getting the walls down. Many people want to just get right with God, but not with their brothers and sisters. Yet there must be transparency. "Nothing between my soul and the Saviour, nothing between my soul and my brother," is the theme song of revival.

Joy and Peace

There is always joy in the camp when revival comes. The Psalmist prayed in Psalm 85:6, *"Wilt Thou not revive us again: that thy people may rejoice in thee?"* There is unspeakable joy when the power of God is upon a people. There is a holy epidemic of joy when God's people begin to forgive one another. One of sin's consequences is turmoil both inwardly and outwardly. But when the joy of forgiving comes, along with it comes peace.

Jesus said, *"My peace I leave with you, My peace I give unto you" (John 14:27)*. Matthew Henry had an interesting comment on the peace the Lord Jesus gives. He wrote:

> When Christ was about to leave this world, He made His will. His soul He committed to His Father; His body He bequeathed to Joseph to be decently interred; His clothes fell to the soldiers; His mother was left to the care of John. But what should He leave His poor disciples? He had no silver or gold, but He left them that which was infinitely better—His peace![2]

Edwin Markum was a poet who made a good living writing. He had a friend who was also a banker to whom he entrusted the management of his finances for retirement. When Markum neared retirement, he discovered that his banker friend had misused the money and in fact had lost it all. He felt wounded and betrayed. He had nothing on which to retire. It burned within him until he hated the man. He would not forgive him. He knew that he must go back to work. Attempting to write, he would sit at his desk for days and nothing would come. His creative juices had been poisoned and paralyzed by bitterness. Finally one day as he sat at his desk aimlessly making circles on a piece of paper, he realized, "If I don't forgive this man, I will destroy myself." He bowed his head and prayed, "O God, O God, help me; I do forgive him." Instantly the burden lifted and he penned these words:

> He drew a circle that shut me out;
> Heretic, rebel, a thing to flout.
> But love and I had the will to win--
> We drew a circle that took him in.

Edwin Markum went on to write for 20 more years and they were the most productive of his life, because he forgave!

Romans 12:18 admonishes, *"If it be possible, as much as lieth in you, live peaceably with **all men**."* Jesus said, *"Blessed are the peacemakers."* We are to do all within us by God's grace to live in peace and harmony with others. There may be times when the other party is not willing to make peace. When this occurs, claim your freedom and move on. Refuse to be trapped in bondage by the reactions of others over which you have no control. Do right and leave the matter with God. Forgiveness yields the blessed and holy fruit of joy and peace—within and without. Some of God's finest gifts become ours when in obedience we forgive as Christ forgave.

Questions For Personal Growth

What Are the Contagious Fruits of Forgiving?

1. Based on the fruits of forgiveness, prepare a written testimony from your own recent experience of obedience in either granting or seeking forgiveness. Consider allowing your pastor to read it, and asking him to permit you to share the testimony with the congregation.

2. What should be your response if someone from whom you sought forgiveness reacted harshly to you or refused to forgive you? Ponder the teaching of Proverbs 16:7 in this connection: *"When a man's ways please the Lord, he maketh even his enemies to be at peace with him."*

[1] John MacArthur, Jr., *The Elements of Church Discipline* (Panorama City, CA: Word of Grace Communications, 1984), p. 87.

[2] Matthew Henry, *Matthew Henry's Commentary* (Old Tappan, NJ: Fleming H. Revell Company), Vol. V. p. 1119.

Chapter 15

Has God Forgiven You?

God's goal in the forgiveness He provides through Christ is that of reconciliation. The word reconcile means "to be at peace with." When we were enemies, we were reconciled to God by the death of His Son (Rom. 5:10). Our old sin nature is opposed to God. The Bible states that the fleshly nature is warring against God (Romans 8:7). When God forgives the repentant sinner, He reconciles that one who was His enemy before forgiveness. There is no longer a division. The forgiven sinner is at peace with God—reconciled.

Christ's death on Calvary was God's way of paying our debt of offense against a Holy God. Man's sin brought the penalty of death. Our sin debt had to be paid. Christ took this debt upon Himself. He satisfied the debt fully by personally bearing the loss. The Lord Jesus took our sin and its penalty in His own body on the Cross. Jesus did not ignore or overlook our debt. He paid the ultimate price by dying in our place and totally satisfying God's justice. Before sinners could be forgiven, sin had to be judged.

The debt had to be satisfied. Through Christ's death, the payment has been made and God is satisfied. There is one thing God could never accept for sin and that is an excuse. Your sin will either be pardoned in Christ or judged eternally in Hell. In His great love and mercy, God has provided the way of forgiveness in His Son.

Alexander the Czar of Russia used to camp with his soldiers right on the field. One night after everything was quiet and dark, he was walking across the camp among the tents and saw a light in an officer's tent. It was very late as he went up to the tent and lifted the flap. He noticed the young officer sitting at the table with his head down on his arms as the candle burned. Alexander went into the tent and noticed that in his hand the officer had a revolver. He was sound asleep. He began to read the piece of paper on the table. There was a long list of debts. He recognized this boy as a son of the nobility of Russia. At the bottom where the soldier had added up the sum of his debts, he wrote, "Who can pay so much?" The Czar figured out that the son was in a position where he could not pay the debt, and rather than disgrace his family and name, he would take his own life. He picked up the pen and under the question "Who can pay so much?" he wrote, "Alexander." He left and soon the young man awakened and picked up the revolver to end his life. As he did, he looked at the list one more time and read down through it, getting even more despairing all the time. But at the bottom of the list he read, "Alexander." He recognized the signature of the Czar and leaped up from the table and cried, "I'm saved!"

Who could pay so much for our sins? The Lord Jesus. He suffered in our place, taking our blame upon Himself even though He was innocent. Christ paid a debt He did not owe because we had a debt we could not pay.

When men repent of their sins and trust in Jesus Christ,

they have peace with God. What grace, that we as aliens and enemies may hear God speak peace to our hearts. How do you receive the forgiveness of God? You must come to God with a broken heart over your sinfulness, realizing it is impossible for you to pay your own debt. You cry out to God for mercy, acknowledging that what you deserve is eternal judgment. And in the midst of your brokenness, God comes in tender grace and forgives your debt. There is only one picture in all the Bible of God running, and that is the picture of the father running to forgive and receive his erring child (Luke 15).

It may be that you, like most people, have been deeply hurt by someone. Perhaps it is even a family member or spouse. It may be a friend or work associate who has somehow offended you. For years, you have been waiting for that person to change. It may be that God is waiting for you to change. Forgiveness cannot be drummed up. It is only as you receive from God for yourself His acceptance and forgiveness of you for what is in your own heart that you can find forgiveness flowing from within you to others. You may find that you are the one who has in fact done the hurting rather than your having been hurt so much. Perhaps you are rejecting, unloving, indifferent, and doing the very things you thought were being done to you. As you confess your sins to the Lord there can be a broken heart over your own sinfulness. It is much easier to be brokenhearted over the sins of others than broken-hearted over your own sins, isn't it?

It is only as you take from God through Christ His forgiveness that you will find the release you desire and must have. God allows hurts and offenses to come into our lives because there is something He wants to do in us to heal us. The very person you react to may be the one God has chosen to use to heal a part of you that so desperately needs His touch.

Picture the Lord Jesus Christ beside you right now, and beside Him that person who has hurt you most deeply. Hear Him say to you, "I love you and I died for you and everything you've ever done. Will you take My forgiveness? And I know how much this person has hurt you. Will you forgive them for My sake? Instead of focusing on how this one has hurt you so, will you not look into your own heart and see what I see there, and let Me forgive you and love and accept you?"

What would be your response to Him? How you respond will determine not only the course of relationships for time, but your eternal destiny as well.

Questions For Personal Growth

Has God Forgiven You?

1. What is the basis of God's forgiveness?
2. If you were asked to describe how one may receive the forgiveness of God, what would you say?
3. If you have never turned from sin, recognizing your offenses against a Holy God, and trusted in Christ as your Saviour, do so now as God speaks to your heart.

Chapter 16

How Do I Know I Have Forgiven?

A portion of the familiar "Lord's Prayer" goes as follows: *"Forgive us our trespasses as we forgive those who trespass against us."* If the Lord were to forgive you today in the same way that you are forgiving other people, how would you be forgiven? Perhaps you would not be receiving much of His forgiveness on those terms. Allow this truth to penetrate your heart. None of us has the power within ourselves to forgive. We must cry out, "Lord, you never said I could; You always said You would. Please do the work of forgiving in me and through me." God never asks anything of you except what His grace puts into you. He never commands without giving the ability to carry it out.

How can you know you have really forgiven another? The ultimate question is simply this: Is God bigger than your hurt? Or will you allow your hurt to be bigger than your God? Ultimately, you will choose the answer for your own life.

It is easy to love God because He is perfect. It is not so

easy to love others, because none of us even comes close to perfection. As one wit put it, "To dwell there above with those that we love, that will be Glory. To dwell here below with those that we know, that's another story!" This is precisely why the Lord said that we will know He is Who He is because of our love for one another. There is nothing natural about that. It is supernatural.

In those times when we are literally consumed with the hurt done to us, we must choose to believe that God's Word is truer than anything we feel. We must obey God and choose to forgive, allowing God in His own time to bring our emotions in line. Be aware that it may take months for your emotions to come in line with truth.

Five Stages of Forgiveness

Just about the time you think this thing of forgiving is solidly under your belt, something will come to your life which will devastate you. You may do all that you know to do, reckon on all the truth you have, and it will not seem to work. The pain may become desperate and there will seem to be no way out.

It is a very arresting fact that just as there are five stages to death and dying, we may identify five states to forgiveness. Forgiveness is a death—death to self.

Concerning death and dying, the first stage is that of denial. We deny the reality of our own death when faced with it. Secondly, there is anger. We blame others for allowing death to destroy us. The third stage is bargaining. Conditions are set up which must be fulfilled before we are ready to die. The fourth is depression. We blame ourselves for letting death destroy us. Finally, there is acceptance. We look forward to dying.

It is incredible that we go through these same five stages when we are hurt. The first stage is not to admit we are hurt. Secondly, we blame others for hurting us. We then set up conditions which must be met before we will forgive. We blame ourselves for letting others hurt us. And fifth, we learn to look forward to growth from hurt.

It is helpful to know that one may become stuck in one of these stages, particularly the anger and depression stages. A person who is dying physically can work through the stages by accepting his feelings and sharing them with someone who will listen in a non-judgmental way. In the same way, when a person is "dying from forgiveness" it can be helpful to express our feelings to the Lord, out loud. This is precisely what the Psalmist does in so many passages. When we do this, like the Psalmist, we begin to hear the sinfulness of our own heart and we are pierced by the truth. We will recognize in this way that what is coming out of our lips is not the fruit of the Spirit.

To Forgive Or Not To Forgive

One deacon fell out with another deacon and the two carried the grudge for years. Finally, the old deacon was upon his deathbed. Some of the brethren came to talk with him. They said, "Look, brother, you are about to die. You don't want to meet God this way. Why don't you forgive your brother?" The deacon asked, "Are you sure I'm dying?" The church leaders replied in the affirmative— the doctors gave him only a matter of days. "Now, get it right," they exhorted. The deacon responded, "Well, you go tell him I forgive him, but I want you to know that if I get well, it's all off." This will never do! What are some tests to determine the genuiness of our forgiving?

First, are you able to **actively, seriously pray for the person you have forgiven?** Of course, the prayer may get stuck in your throat, but you must purpose in your heart that you will pray for him or her every time he comes to mind. Can you pray and desire God's best for him?

Secondly, **break down the word forgiveness.** Ask yourself, "Am I looking FOR-a-way-of-GIVING to you? Or am I withholding in my heart?" If you are withholding in your heart, you do not have the spirit of forgiveness God expects. Can you make an investment of some sort in the one you have forgiven? Can you give to them something of value to you? This will prove not only to yourself, but also to them the sincerity of your forgiveness. The greatest investment you may make is that of acceptance. This will mean you can no longer judge them, criticize them in your heart, or express to them your disapproval by looks or by words. True forgiveness trusts the other person and is even willing to open itself to being hurt again. This response will often bring a new spirit toward you and healing will take place.

Mark Twain said, "Forgiveness is the fragrance of the violet on the heel of the one who crushed it." If someone hurts you and crushes you, when they walk away from you, it should be as though that person stepped on a violet. To forgive is to cancel the debt as though it never happened, to wipe the slate clean. This is a fragrance many in our world desperately need to smell.

A third test of forgiveness comes **when you hear something detrimental about the one you have professed to forgive.** Does your heart secretly rejoice over such news? Scripture tells us that this attitude displeases the Lord (Prov. 24:17). Delighting over his calamity proves you have not reconciled him and made peace in your own heart.

When you meet this individual on the street, or at church, or pass him on the highway, **what are the thoughts which enter your heart concerning him?** This is a fourth test of forgiveness. While the human mind is not like a computer bank which can have information erased from it, still the knowledge of the hurt having occurred does not evoke the same hostility as before. Forgiveness has cleansed their record in your heart. You find both the desire and the freedom to love the former offender and wish him well.

Fifth, can you honestly ask the Lord, **"What qualities are You wanting to build into my life through this hurt?"** Can you be genuine enough to seek the counsel of the person you have forgiven should the Lord prompt your heart that a blindspot on your part was involved? If so, this is a clear indication of spiritual maturity and of unpretentious forgiveness.

Forgiveness is the way of the Cross. It is the way of death. It is also the way of life abundant in Christ. The road to perfection or spiritual maturity is often painful because its means are contrary to our human nature. But God never speaks in vague, idealistic generalities. He is to be taken seriously. C.S. Lewis, in <u>Mere Christianity</u> sets it forth well.

> When He said, "Be perfect," He meant it. He meant that we must go in for the full treatment. It is hard; but the sort of compromise we are all hankering after is harder—in fact, it is impossible. It may be hard for an egg to turn into a bird: it would be a jolly sight harder for it to learn to fly while remaining in the egg. We are like eggs at present. And you cannot go on indefinitely being just an ordinary, decent egg. We must be hatched or go bad . . . . If we let Him—for we can prevent Him, if we choose—He will make the feeblest and filthiest of us into . . . a dazzling, radiant, immortal creature, pulsating all through with such energy

and joy and wisdom and love as we cannot now imagine, a bright stainless mirror which reflects back to God perfectly (though of course, on a smaller scale) His own boundless power and delight and goodness. The process will be long and in parts very painful; but that is what we are in for. Nothing less.[1]

He meant what He said. Forgiveness—the mandate of God, the way of the Cross, the key to human relationships, the joy of growth and victorious living, and the way to get along with everybody . . . all the time.

Questions For Personal Growth

How Do I Know I Have Forgiven?

1. Consider the impact of the following statement from this chapter: "In those times when we are literally consumed with the hurt done to us, we must choose to believe that God's Word is truer than anything we feel." How would this statement apply to your response toward someone, who, for example, had murdered a loved one of yours?

2. Someone has observed that "God has never used anyone greatly until He has first hurt him deeply." What is God's ultimate purpose in allowing others to hurt, offend, or wrong us? How does our response to hurts affect the working out of God's purpose in our lives?

3. The chapter mentions five stages of forgiving. At what stage are you in regard to the deepest hurt you have ever experienced? As needed, seek the Lord to enable you to go on to the growth stage.

4. Honestly determine the answers to the tests of your forgiveness:

— Can you pray for the one you forgave? Do so now.
— Will you make some sort of investment in the life of that person?
— What is your first thought upon hearing something negative about a person you forgave?
— What is your first thought when you meet one you have forgiven?

[1]C. S. Lewis, *Mere Christianity* (Westwood, NJ: Barbour and Company, by special arrangement with Macmillan Incorporated), pp. 168, 174.

Further Resources
on the
Vital Subject of Forgiveness

Harold Vaughan is the founder and president of Christ Life Ministries. Evangelist and revivalist, Harold and his family travel extensively to local churches throughout the United States and Canada conducting Spiritual Life Crusades. Forgiveness and reconciliation are absolutely essential when it comes to personal and corporate revival. Harold's message "Forgiveness" is available on tape.

VIDEO AND CASSETTE TAPES

Forgiveness
What is forgiveness? How can I forgive? Can I be freed from the bitterness and anger that is in my heart? These practical and relevant questions are thoroughly dealt with in this popular crusade message. This sermon on forgiveness has brought lasting help to many. Pastors utilize this message as a tool for counseling those caught in the gall of bitterness.

Video — $18.95 postpaid
Cassette — $5.00 postpaid

Order yours today from the
order blank on the last page.

Other Titles From
Christ Life Publications

PRINCIPLES OF SPIRITUAL GROWTH by Miles Stanford. Each chapter in this classic is a masterpiece. Chapter titles include "Faith," "Time," "Appropriation," "Identification," "The Cross," "Rest," "Cultivation," etc. "Not I, but Christ" is the simple, yet profound message of this easy-to-read volume. Regardless of where you are in your spiritual journey, this book will be a blessing to your soul!

THE NATURE OF A GOD-SENT REVIVAL by Duncan Campbell. Will it be business as usual or the unusual business of revival? This powerful booklet is packed with power from a man who saw spiritual awakening in his ministry. Thousands were converted when God stepped down from Heaven in the Hebrides.

SINNERS IN THE HANDS OF AN ANGRY GOD by Jonathan Edwards. This is the most famous sermon ever preached. People in the congregation were gripped in terror as Jonathan Edwards delivered this alarming message. Order several copies TODAY for you and friends!

"LORD, HELP ME NOT TO HAVE THESE EVIL THOUGHTS!" by Harold Vaughan. Quite often Christians pray this prayer, but instead of the thoughts ceasing, they only intensify. Here's a practical guide to achieving a healthy thought-life while engaged in mental warfare.

WHAT IT MEANS TO BE CRUCIFIED WITH CHRIST by Harold Vaughan. What did Paul mean in Galatians 2:20: "I am crucified with Christ"? Here are twelve brief and readable chapters on the "exchanged life" along with many helpful charts and study guides.

*Write today and request an up-to-date CLP Product Guide!

Order Form for FORGIVENESS:
How to Get Along With Everybody All the Time!

Quantity Prices/U.S. Funds
1 Copy $5.95 each plus $1.50 handling
5 Copies $4.95 each plus $2.00 handling
10 Copies $4.00 each plus $4.00 handling
25 Copies $3.50 each plus $5.00 handling
50 Copies $2.50 each plus $7.50 handling

Quantity   **Total**

_____ *Forgiveness: How to Get Along With*
Everybody All the Time! $5.95 .... $ _____

_____ Forgiveness Video $18.95 ....

_____ Forgiveness Cassette $5.00 .... $ _____

_____ *The Principles of Spiritual Growth*
by Miles Stanford $4.95 .... $ _____

_____ *The Nature of a God-Sent Revival*
by Duncan Campbell $1.95 .... $ _____

_____ *Sinners in the Hands of an Angry God*
by Jonathan Edwards $1.95 .... $ _____

_____ *"Lord, Help Me Not to Have These*
Evil Thoughts!" $4.99 .... $ _____

_____ *What It Means to Be Crucified With*
Christ $2.95 .... $ _____

VA residents add 4-1/2% sales tax .... $ _____

Postage **(Minimum $1.50)** .... $ _____

Total .... $ _____

Make checks payable to: **Christ Life Publications**
P.O. Box 399, Vinton, VA 24179

Name _____

Address _____

City, State, Zip _____